KEEPING AND BREEDING TORTOISES IN CAPTIVITY

A.C. HIGHFIELD

R&A

1990

First Edition 1990
Published and Distributed by
  R & A Publishing Limited
  3 Highfield Villas
  Newlands Hill
  Portishead, Avon
  England BS20 9AU.

ISBN 1 872688 01 2 (soft-cover)

Front Cover: *Geochelone pardalis*

Photoset, printed and bound in Great Britain by
The Longdunn Press Ltd, Bristol

Contents

Preface

This book has been prepared in response to the very many requests I have received from tortoise enthusiasts around the world for an accessible, practical and comprehensive guide to breeding tortoises in captivity. I hope however to show that the technology of captive breeding can also make an invaluable contribution to conservation; not only by encouraging enthusiasts to breed their animals in captivity rather than by sourcing them from the wild (thus depleting natural populations) but also by enabling critically endangered populations to be replenished by the careful application of the same techniques.

It is not necessarily all that difficult to breed tortoises; provided one has a well matched pair, maintains them under reasonable conditions, and provides basic incubation facilities nature will often contribute the rest. It is however difficult to breed tortoises well, and to breed them consistently. It is a fact that many captive breeding programs – both amateur and professional – end in disaster. Very often the reasons for this are poor genetic selection, poor incubation techniques and poor dietary management of the hatchlings. I have attempted to cover each of these points in this book, and to demonstrate how the most common mistakes can be avoided.

This is above all a practical guide, and one based upon first hand experience of breeding and maintaining a very wide range of tortoise species in captivity as well as extensive work with tortoises in the field – from the Galapagos Islands to the Mediterranean. Despite that, I would be the very first to admit that there is much that we do not really know about these ancient and enigmatic reptiles; much of their pre-history remains shrouded in mystery, and certain aspects of their biology and reproductive behaviour are even today only beginning to be understood.

The successful maintenance of tortoises in captivity poses many challenges to keepers. It is fair to say that with their very specific environmental and dietary requirements, tortoises are in fact one of the more difficult reptiles to manage. Many times I have been consulted by zoos with requests for advice on some aspect or other relating to the 'common' tortoises in their collection; these it usually turns out are consigned to some corner of the 'pet' animal section, set well apart from the 'real' reptiles! And yet, whereas these same zoos consistently breed their snakes and lizards, and keep specimens alive and in good health for very many years, their breeding successes with the 'common' tortoises are often far from consistent and there is a higher mortality rate among the tortoises than almost any other reptile in the collection. I only mention this to stress that even experienced and professional reptile keepers do not find tortoises easy animals to sustain and breed consistently under captive conditions.

To find the reasons for this, one has only to look at how intimately wild tortoises rely upon their natural environment for all of their biological requirements; food, warmth, moisture, humidity, light, cover, nesting sites and mates are all there in exactly the right balance. Tortoises are 'niche' animals which have adapted over the millennia to fit perfectly into a very specific environmental and ecological 'slot'. Remove them from that environment, cut them off from their ecological roots, and tortoises very rapidly begin to experience serious difficulties. Most captive environments do not even begin to approach the true environmental and ecological ideal of the animals they are supposed to contain. It is for this reason – because it is so absolutely fundamental to successful maintenance – that I would suggest that everyone who wishes to keep tortoises in captivity should examine as carefully as possible the native habitats of whatever species they intend to keep. Nothing is more instructive, or is likely to provide more insight, than a few days spent meeting tortoises in the wild or in visiting their habitats.

Tortoises – and turtles – are very sensitive animals. Anyone who desires to succeed with them must first come to understand them. I have been more fortunate than most in that my work for the Tortoise Trust, and latterly also for the Tortoise Survival Project has enabled me to maintain close contact with tortoises around the world on a daily basis for a number of years. In that time I have never ceased to be amazed by their 'at oneness' with their natural environments and by their remarkable tenacity to survive even under very extreme conditions. I started out by being merely curious about them; I have ended up full of admiration for them.

Tortoises today face an uncertain future in a rapidly changing world. They are archaic creatures whose destiny is bound up with that of the habitats they occupy. If they are to have any future at all, then the protection and conservation of those habitats is essential. I am encouraged by the increasing awareness of the need for habitat conservation generally, and also by the enthusiasm of tortoise and turtle keepers around the world who are more than ever before taking an active role in chelonian conservation. Whether by campaigning for the protection of fragile habitats, by offering support to projects working to protect tortoises or by creating a self-sustaining captive population which no longer relies upon wild-caught animals the individual keeper can make a significant contribution.

Chapter One

The role of captive breeding

The ultimate objective of most serious and conservation conscious reptile keepers is to achieve consistent and sustainable captive reproduction; only in this way can we really justify the keeping of rare or endangered species in captivity. Breeding threatened species of reptile in captivity is increasingly the only method by which fellow enthusiasts can obtain specimens; it is no longer acceptable to make extensive collections in the wild in order to supply this need. Furthermore, the technical knowledge gained in captive breeding projects can contribute greatly to the success of other projects based in the natural habitat.

Captive breeding tortoises or turtles is an extremely challenging undertaking, as these are by no means easy animals to induce to breed successfully and consistently; raising the hatchlings to a healthy adulthood and hopefully to manage these well enough to produce 2nd and 3rd captive-bred generations is if anything an even bigger challenge. Yet with dedication and good management it can be done.

The conservation role which can be played by captive breeding is nowhere better illustrated than on the Galapagos. By the late 1960's the future of the handful of surviving Galapagos Hood island tortoises *Geochelone (Chelonoidis) elephantopus hoodensis* was looking bleak. Thousands had been slaughtered in the 19th Century by visiting whalers (between them, two ships logs record taking 585 tortoises in 1831 alone) and by 1847 the population was effectively decimated. The number of tortoises was reduced to such an extent that even the whalers considered it no longer worth their while to continue the hunt. Scientific search parties in 1906 managed to locate only 3 living tortoises. The population faced total extinction – indeed, some believed that this may already have occurred. Nonetheless, fresh expeditions set out and finally during the 1960's a total of fourteen adults comprising twelve females and two males were located. These were removed to the safety of the Charles Darwin Research Station on Santa Cruz and by 1971 the first eggs were at last successfully incubated.

The Hood island tortoises, along with other races from different islands are now breeding regularly and successfully at the Darwin Station. Reintroductions into the wild of captive reared juveniles are gradually swelling the populations of the most critically endangered races, and the evidence is that survivorship is good. Young tortoises are susceptible to predation not only by natural enemies such as birds, but also by introduced predators such as rats and feral domestic animals. By 'head-starting' hatchlings past the age of peak predation the maximum conservation benefit of captive breeding can be attained.

It is not only on the Galapagos where captive breeding is seen as an answer to the tortoises plight; in the South of France *Testudo hermanni hermanni* is being captive bred by similar means for release into their native habitat. Again, the 'head-start' technique is proving highly successful. Other programs around the world are using similar methods to fend off extinction in critically endangered populations. In Mexico the extremely rare endemic Chihuahuan desert tortoise *Gopherus flavomarginatus* had been hunted for food to such an extent that total extinction was feared within 20 years. An enlightened educational effort involving local people in conservation activities (one of the areas best known ex-tortoise hunters now works for the program) combined with stiff penalties for illegally taking a tortoise has reversed the trend but once again captive breeding holds the most promise for eventualy repopulation. In Madagascar similar efforts are being made on behalf of the beautiful radiated tortoises, *Geochelone (Asterochelys) radiata* and *Geochelone (Asterochelys) yniphora*. Italian Hermann's tortoises meanwhile are about to benefit from Project CARAPAX which intends to breed several thousand 'replacement' tortoises with which to re-populate the countryside.

In Africa, the Tortoise Survival Project is for the first time attempting to assess, and ultimately reverse, some of the damage done by 50 years of intensive trade collecting. It has been estimated that over 1 million tortoises were taken from Morocco alone between 1967 and 1981. Collections were indiscriminate and vast numbers perished en-route to the pet shops of Europe. More died during their first hibernation. The Tortoise Survival Project has recently established that not only *Testudo graeca* Linnaeus 1758 (the typical Moorish land tortoise) but also a very rare species belonging to a different genus; *Furculachelys whitei* Bennett 1836 was included, unrecognised, in this vast trade. This tortoise was named after Gilbert White's famous 'Timothy' tortoise of Selborne, first

2

described in 1836 and thereafter forgotten about until re-discovered by the Project in 1989 – exactly 200 years after the first publication of White's 'Natural History'. A urgent effort is now underway to save it and similar recently discovered rare endemic forms from eventual extinction. Captive breeding will play an important role.

The core of all these programs is essentially the same. A small breeding stock of endangered tortoises is removed to a safe area where eggs can be laid without risk of the nests being attacked by predators (human or animal). In some programs it is possible to simply protect the nests by means of wire mesh and allow incubation to occur naturally, in the ground. At other times it is preferable to remove the eggs from the nest once the female has finished laying and place them in an artificial incubator whilst development takes place. In many wild situations, egg predation can affect up to 80% of all nests with wild pigs, foxes and pine martens being particularly effective and systematic predators. These attrition rates can be reduced to nil by artificial incubation, thus dramatically boosting the recovery potential of a depressed population.

One particularly crucial problem facing all conservation based captive programs may not be immediately obvious, and that is to ensure that only true pairs are allowed to breed. If random cross-breeding occurs, then an endangered species could literally be bred to the point of extinction. This is where the roles of taxonomist, geneticist, ecologist and zoo keeper can combine to ensure that only the correct species and sub-species are bred and re-introduced into native habitats. No introductions of captive-bred stock should ever be made until the situation has thoroughly investigated and the impact of such an operation very carefully assessed. This form of genetic management must extend not only to the species and sub-species level, but must also be applied at the level of individual populations. Where eventual release of captive bred stock is intended therefore, the genetic integrity of populations must be maintained.

Genetics and cross breeding

For obvious reasons it is undesirable to produce offspring from differing species; fortunately in the case of tortoises, it is also (usually) extremely difficult. Despite looking for evidence of successful cross-matings for several years, I have only ever encountered a few genuine cases at first hand. Most cases of alleged hybridisation reported to us and subsequently investigated were based upon simple mis-identification of the parents, others upon pre-fertilisation of a female by a male of identical type but subsequently mated by male of a different species which was then assumed to be a parent. The sometimes very extended gestation periods of

3

tortoises between conception and laying frequently leads to this type of mistake. Some hybridisation may indeed occur naturally between some geographically adjacent races, and it may be possible to induce it between normally widely separated races when both are held in captivity. Any such instances must be regarded as unusual and certainly the physical construction of some species, the size of their eggs and unique biotypic adaptions would suggest that such reports must be treated with skepticism until carefully verified.

There are reports in the literature of cross-breeding between *Testudo marginata* and *Testudo ibera* (both of which occur in Greece), and also of hybridisation between *Testudo hermanni* and *Testudo horsfieldi*; In one case I have observed cross-bred hatchlings from (non-sympatric) Turkish *T. ibera* and n. African *T. graeca*. The most curious feature was that in both of these cases the hatchlings appeared to inherit all their visible (external) characters from the male, and displayed no characters whatsoever typical of the female or indeed did not demonstrate any other combination of traits to suggest that cross-breeding had occurred. This is certainly an extremely interesting result and is now undergoing further investigation. I have also examined cross-bred hatchlings from *T. marginata* and *T. ibera* but in this case characters seemed to be inherited from both parents in approximately equal proportions. It is also a point worth noting that whilst cross-matings very rarely produce fertile eggs, almost any mating activity seems to stimulate females to generate eggs – even though where genetically disparate animals are involved these are more often than not infertile.

Much definitely remains to be discovered in respect of chelonian speciation and genetics; however, for all practical purposes the following guidelines should suffice:

✳ Do not deliberately induce cross-matings between different species or sub-species. Fertility is likely to be nil or very greatly reduced and the offspring may be infertile. It is also ecologically damaging to produce such hybrids.

✳ Do not breed from siblings or from closely related pairs. Inbreeding suppression, although not an immediate consequence, may occur in the long term when such practices are sustained.

✳ Introduce new genetic input into any captive breeding program frequently by means of breeding loans and exchanges etc.

✳ Never release captive bred stock into wild habitats. Any such releases should only occur after the most exhaustive scientific studies and preferably even then only after DNA or genetic screening has confirmed that it is safe to do so.

∗ If at all possible, maintain animals from individual populations separately and breed only from truly compatible pairs from similar genetic and zoogeographic backgrounds. Keep careful records of all resulting hatchlings.

Finally, do not assume that the taxonomic nomenclature and status of tortoises is fully understood and is fixed. It is not. Taxonomy is a continually developing science. Until only recently, for example, it was thought that only a single species (*Testudo graeca* L. 1758) occurred throughout north Africa – this has subsequently proved to be far from the case. Similarly, a 'miniature' race of *Testudo marginata* Schoepff 1792 (the Marginated tortoise) has only very recently been discovered which may require separate designation as a geographic sub-species. Similar conditions apply to many species; *Geochelone (Chelonoidis) carbonaria*, *Geochelone (Chelonoidis) chilensis*, *Kinixys belliana* and *Testudo hermanni* are all highly complex taxonomic units which are formed of many individual populations, some demonstrating a great deal of individual variety and divergence. It is highly likely that certain of these taxa will, on further investigation, prove to comprise more than one 'simple' species.

The message for those intending to captive breed tortoises is therefore very clear – treat all taxa with caution, and if possible, base captive breeding colonies not simply upon currently accepted taxonomic divisions (which may change!) but on geographic populations. Not only is this approach consistently the most successful, but it avoids any possibility of 'genetic pollution'.

Sexual maturity & age of breeding stock

Careful observations on a wide range of species indicate that primarily physical size rather than age is the indicator and initiator of sexual maturity in tortoises. Size is of course related to age but as captive-bred specimens often grow much faster that equivalent wild specimens (due to the normally better availability of food) these often mature sexually and attain breeding capability much earlier than their wild counterparts. For example, in the wild *T. graeca* and *G. pardalis* usually mature at approximately 15 years of age – captive bred examples can easily mature at less than half this, in 6–8 years. In one instance, we know of the successful mating of an adult female *G. pardalis* by a 4 year old male.

At the other end of the scale, extreme caution should be exercised in attempting to use elderly female tortoises for captive breeding purposes.

5

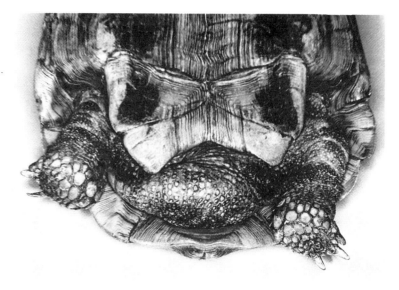

Male *Testudo hermanni*; note long tail and rear plastral lobe shape.

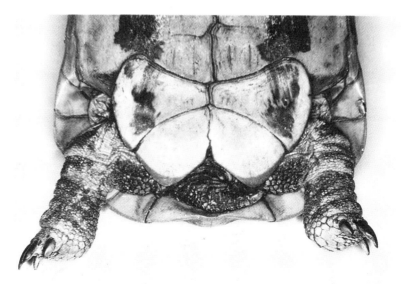

Female *T. hermanni*; note short tail and different rear plastral lobe shape.

Female (left) and male (right) Leopard tortoises.

Where eggs have not been produced for many years severe obstetric difficulties can ensue. In our own captive breeding programs all elderly female tortoises are automatically excluded and are maintained separately from the males to avoid undue stress or the danger of egg retention.

Sexual dimorphism in tortoises

In most species of tortoise it is comparatively easy to determine the sex of specimens by using the following primary sexual characteristics;

Tail length – In mature males the tail is almost always longer than that of females.

Plastron – In many species the plastron of males is deeply curved or indented.

Size – In most species, adult males are considerably smaller than adult females.

There are, in addition to these primary characters, a large number of secondary characters specific to individual species; often these are difficult to evaluate until considerable experience has been gained. Even

Female (left) and male (right) Redfoot tortoises.

Redfoot tortoises; the female (left) has a wider, flatter plastron than the male (right) and a much shorter tail.

8

the above primary characters are not universally applicable – for example, the plastrons of some male *Geochelone pardalis* (the Leopard tortoise) are as flat as those of females, there is very little difference in tail length between male and female *Geochelone (Chelonoidis) chilensis* (the Chaco tortoise) and male *Geochelone (Chelonoidis) elephantopus* (Galapagos tortoises) are usually very much larger than females. However, the above guidelines do hold true for the majority of species likely to be encountered. Major dimorphic characters within individual species are discussed in the chapter dealing with identification and breeding notes.

Sexual behaviour

The detail of courtship behaviour does vary between species; often quite considerably. *Geochelone (Chelonoidis) carbonaria* (Redfoot tortoises), for example, engage in a strange pre-nuptial head nodding ritual where the male extends his neck and rapidly shakes his head up and down whilst making a unique 'clucking' noise; something similar (but without the accompanying noise) is seen in *Testudo horsfieldi*. North African *Testudo graeca* and trans-caucasian *Testudo ibera* violently ram and butt the females prior to mating; in *Testudo hermanni* ramming behaviour is rarely seen, but head and leg biting is commonplace. Mating males frequently emit species characteristic sounds – these sounds are so unique to each species that it is possible for experienced observers to identify them merely by listening to a tape recording of the various vocalisations.

For obvious physical reasons the mating postures adopted by the various species of land tortoises are all very similar. The male assumes a mounted position, the tail probes for and locates the females cloacal opening. The males engorged penis is then inserted into the cloaca of the female. One of the more unusual postures is that employed by Box Tortoises of the genus *Terrapene*.

Clutch size and egg dimensions

Land tortoises are by no means as prolific in egg production as marine turtles. The number of eggs laid in a clutch also varies considerably between species – from 1 single egg in the case of *Malacochersus tornieri* (the Pancake tortoise) to 20 or more eggs per clutch in *Geochelone pardalis* (table 1). Egg size also differs between species as table 2 shows. Fertility within clutches is usually high, at about 80% on average in most species. In the wild between 50% and 90% of hatchlings fail to reach adult breeding age due to predation and other causes. In captivity, with careful management, juvenile mortality can be reduced to practically nil.

9

Table 1 - Comparative average clutch densities

Typical quantity	Species	Average clutches per year
1 egg:	*Malacochersus, Chersina* spp.	3-7.
2 eggs:	*Psammobates* spp.	1 or more.
4-8 eggs:	*T. graeca, T. hermanni,* *G. carbonaria, Terrapene* spp, *Kinixys* spp.	2.
5-10 eggs:	*T. ibera, T. marginata,* *Gopherus* & *Xerobates* spp.	2 or more.
8-15 eggs:	*Furculachelys* spp.	2 or more.
10-25 eggs:	*Geochelone pardalis.*	3-7.

Egg size and shape differs between species; *Testudo ibera* (left), elongate egg of *T. hermanni boettgeri* (right).

10

Table 2 – Typical egg dimensions

Species	Length	Width
Testudo ibera	36.00mm	30.00mm
T. h. hermanni	29.75mm	24.00mm
T. h. boettgeri	40.00mm	29.25mm
F. whitei	33.00mm	27.50mm
T. g. graeca	30.00mm	27.50mm
T. marginata	30.50mm	28.00mm
T. horsfieldi	47.00mm	34.00mm
T. kleinmanni	29.00mm	23.00mm
G. p. babcocki	43.00mm	43.00mm
G. berlandieri	48.00mm	35.00mm
X. agassizi	44.00mm	39.00mm
G. carbonaria	45.00mm	42.00mm
K. b. belliana	48.00mm	38.00mm
M. tornieri	47.00mm	31.00mm
T. c. carolina	32.00mm	20.00mm

In many cases egg sizes differ not only between species, but also between geographical sub-species; this is most graphically illustrated in the case of *T. hermanni*.

Chapter Two

Eggs & incubation

Most tortoise eggs have a very similar structure although the shape and size may vary considerably from species to species (table 2). They are formed from calcium carbonate in the form of aragonite rather than from calcite as found in bird eggs. The ratio of shell to yolk and albumen is also much higher than that found in birds - typically 16% in tortoises as opposed to a typical figure of 12% for most birds. The eggs of *Testudo graeca* for example consist on average of 44% albumen, 40% yolk and 16% shell. there is a thick fibrous membrane between the inner surface of the shell and albumen. Shortly after laying contraction of the yolk and other contents causes an air cell to appear, usually at one end. This effect can be seen quite clearly if the egg is examined under a bright light source.

Eggs are usually round although some species produce elongate forms. In general large species tend to produce spherical eggs and small species to produce more elongate eggs. The thickness and resilience of the shell wall also varies between species from the parchment-like thin and soft shell of *Terrapene carolina* to the very hard and resilient eggs of *Testudo graeca*.

Even the hardest of tortoise egg shells are permeable to a certain degree; measurements of *Testudo graeca* eggs incubated at 30° C in a dry environment revealed weight losses of between 10%–50% as a result of evaporation over a 12 week incubation period. This weight loss is interesting in that it contrasts directly with the situation pertaining to many other species of reptile some of which actually increase in weight over their incubation period by as much as 70% (e.g cobra eggs increase not only in weight but also in size).

Incubation humidity

In tests conducted by the author, it was observed that fertile eggs dehydrated the least whilst infertile eggs dehydrated the most. After 8

12

weeks at 30° C in a very dry incubation environment it became relatively easy to detect which eggs were fertile and which infertile by weighing them on a set of electronic digital scales. For example one batch of 7 eggs produced 4 fertile eggs which after 8 weeks all weighed between 11.25g and 13.00g and 3 infertile eggs which weighed between 6.00g and 5.00g. Comparative studies produced the further result that at least in the case of *Testudo graeca* no difference in hatching rates were noted irrespective of whether the incubation humidity was low (30%), moderate (50%–60%) or high (80%+). However, infertile eggs dehydrated much more rapidly at lower humidities.

It is probable that the formation of the various membranes and other tissue within fertile eggs serves to conserve internal fluids, and that the reason infertile eggs dehydrate so acutely is that lacking such membranes there is less of a barrier to the migration of fluids. It would seem that fertile hard shelled eggs are relatively immune to variations in incubation humidity, at least within the limits tested. Nonetheless, it is probably sensible not to incubate at either extreme of humidity, just in case. Our experiments all took place within an incubator which had very little airflow over the eggs – we have since received reports that attempts at incubating *T. graeca* eggs in incubators intended for bird eggs have failed due to embryonic dehydration. The airflow in such incubators is much higher than that of our own reptile egg incubators and we feel that this factor was responsible.

Oxygen and the developing embryo

The eggshell is not only permeable to water but also to respiratory and other gasses and this performs important metabolic functions during embryonic development. When this requirement is ignored in artificial incubation, deaths from anoxia must be considered a distinct possibility. The practice of incubating eggs in totally airtight containers is therefore to be strongly discouraged. Whilst it is easier to maintain high levels of humidity in a sealed environment tests have shown that CO_2 levels accumulate rapidly in such situations. Embryonic anoxia is quite possibly the hidden factor responsible for many "dead-in-shell" and premature hatchlings encountered by captive breeders where other explanations (e.g incubator failure or genetic incompatibility) can be discounted.

Where a sealed incubation environment has been used and high levels of mortality encountered, a change to a more natural and aerated incubation method will often produce an immediate and dramatic improvement in survivorship. It is a myth that because eggs are buried underground they require no oxygen or do not need to ventilate waste gasses – in fact, soil oxygen levels of nesting sites are usually good and permeability comparatively high.

Developing tortoise and turtle eggs possess a functional internal lung in the form of the chorio-allantoic membrane – this allows gaseous exchange to occur through the eggshell. CO_2 is produced which must be expirated and fresh oxygen must be obtained from the outside world. In a sealed incubation environment CO_2 builds up and the oxygen supply eventually becomes depleted. A very high mortality is noted, particularly of full-term hatchlings. Survivors may be weak and in some case display evidence of brain damage. Other signs that embryonic anoxia may have occurred include a very high post-hatching mortality and hatchlings leaving the egg carrying excessively large egg-sacs, i.e too early. Certainly if full-term embryos are developing but suffering pre hatching mortality the incubation technique is the most likely causal factor – the only other possibility (a remote one) is a genetic defect. If the problem is occurring with several different species or sets of parents within the same program then the genetic factor is ruled out leaving only incubation technique.

The internal metabolism of the egg

The yolk of chelonian eggs performs the same function as that of bird eggs providing lipoproteins (combined fats and proteins) originally manufactured in the liver of the female and transported via the blood-stream to the oviducts where it is formed into the yolk. In addition to fat and protein the yolk also contains other trace element minerals and vitamins including calcium and phosphorus. However, direct measurements of the calcium content of egg-yolks indicates that these contain insufficient calcium to supply the very heavy calcium demand of an embryonic developing tortoise. In the case of sea-turtles (the chelonian species most intensively studied thus far) the disparity between yolk-calcium and the calcium content of a hatchling is approximately 400%. The excess requirement is met by the osteo-genesis of the calcium tied up in the shell. It is therefore also highly probable that mineral and other nutritional deficiencies in the adult female can seriously impair breeding viability and this will be discussed in some detail later.

After the egg has been fertilised the embryo begins at once to draw upon the yolk for its sustenance. The exact site of fertilisation is unclear but is probably in the ifundibular area. The egg then rapidly moves along the albumen secreting magnum where it is propelled by muscular activity and pulsating hair-like cilia. The function of the albumen is again similar to that of the albumen of birds-eggs, providing fluid support and a small additional reserve of food. Most freshly laid tortoise eggs contain albumen which is gelatinous in parts and extremely fluid in others. Chalazae, the twisted fibrous spirals found in birds eggs are absent in tortoise eggs as they are in all reptilian eggs; most reptiles unlike birds do not "turn" their eggs during incubation and certainly, the lack of chalazae does tend to make the embryo more susceptible to disturbance.

In addition to the main yolk-sac three other important membranes occur within the chelonian egg; the chorion the amnion and allantois. The chorion, which is formed of ectoderm and mesoderm, occurs just beneath the inside surface of the eggshell. The amnion is similarly formed of ectoderm coated with mesoderm and develops into a fluid-filled sac which envelopes the growing embryo. The third membrane, the allantois, forms a receptacle for some of the nitrogenous waste of the embryo including precipitated uric acid and at the point of fusion with the allantois (chorio-allantois) performs the vital function of allowing oxygen and carbon dioxide exchange to take place through the walls of the egg.

Incubation

Incubation in the wild consists of the female selecting a suitable nest site then digging a suitable hole and depositing the eggs leaving nature to do the rest. Although on the surface this may appear perfectly straightforward in reality her task is a complex one. The selected area must comprise earth of the correct texture and humidity. If it is too loose or too stony emerging hatchlings may be trapped and suffocated. If it is too damp the eggs may rot and develop fungal growths (in some species) if too dry they may desiccate. Anyone who has observed female tortoises in search of nest sites will readily attest to the tremendous care taken over the operation. Several 'test' nests are often laboriously excavated then rejected for various reasons. The temperature of the nesting site is perhaps the most critical of all as successful incubation can only occur within a relatively narrow temperature band. The precise mechanisms by which female tortoises select nesting sites remain unclear but this is certainly an area worthy of detailed study.

Temperature measurements taken by the author at nest sites revealed that for *T. graeca* a ground surface temperature of between 38° C and 42° C is often preferred. At approximately 75mm below the surface temperatures of between 27° C and 31° C were recorded at the same sites. In captivity provision of a suitable nest site is extremely important; failure to provide an egg-bearing female with acceptable facilities frequently results in egg-retention and consequent obstetric difficulties. Nesting can take some considerable time – between 1 and 3 hours is average for most species. During this period the female carefully excavates a bell shaped pit with her back legs before laying the clutch in rapid succession. The nest is then filled in, again using the back legs. Once deposited the eggs should be removed for artificial incubation.

As stated above, in the wild nest site selection is obviously very critical and in captivity females usually take equal care. This can present problems as it is not always easy to provide a suitable site which will satisfy her instincts. One special technique which has proved useful with several species where the female seems to be experiencing problems in locating a suitable laying site is to remove her to a separate area with a good depth of substrate of the appropriate type with a 200W spotlamp suspended about 50cm above ground level. The female should be disturbed as little as possible. After a day or two in this environment many otherwise reluctant females will lay without further difficulty.

Chapter Three

Designing & constructing an incubator

Various suggestions for chelonian egg incubators have been published. Some are excellent and well suited to the purpose, others leave much to be desired. The author is strongly opposed to any incubator reliant upon light bulbs for a heat source as these are simply not reliable enough and the constant on-off cycle demanded by incubator use is almost guaranteed to induce filament failure sooner or later. Usually this occurs at the most critical phase of incubation. Fortunately various low cost reliable and safe heaters of suitable design are fairly readily available from electrical and animal hobbyist sources. These can usefully be grouped as follows;

Miniature Industrial Heating Elements: These are generally only available through industrial electronics suppliers and are intended for use in process control, drying cabinets and commercial installations. They may not be easily obtainable through ordinary retail channels, although electronic hobbyist suppliers can sometimes help. Most consist of a low wattage (typically 60–100W) ceramic element contained within a metal shielding. The advantage of such units is their low cost and extremely high reliability. For incubator use they are difficult to better and are definitely my own preferred choice.

Heating Pads: Widely available from exotic animal and aquarium suppliers in a range of sizes and wattage ratings. For use in an incubator a small 35–50W unit is generally more than adequate. The better quality brands are extremely reliable but some cheaper brands are liable to failure so should be avoided.

Submersible Aquarium Heaters: This sort of heater can be useful where it is necessary to maintain very high humidity levels (as in the Type

Heating elements, L to R; miniature industrial heater for type I incubator; 250W infra-red ceramic for vivaria; integral submersible heater-stat for type II incubator.

II incubator discussed below). The heater (typically not more than 60-100W rating) is submerged in a water tray located in the base of the incubator cabinet or heats a water jacket surrounding the incubation media. This type of heating is particularly useful for incubating very soft eggs such as those produced by box-turtles or aquatic chelonia where humidity is especially critical. However it has its dangers. The first and most important point is that should the water tray dry out, overheating of the element will occur very rapidly. At best the element will simply fail. At worst a fire could result.

Incubators for tortoise eggs (and reptile eggs in general) fall into two principle classes; 'dry' incubators and 'wet' incubators.

Type I Incubator design

A highly effective incubator which was designed by the author especially for incubating tortoise eggs which do not require a high incubation humidity is shown on page 19. Although simple to construct this incubator offers very precise temperature regulation and an easy

18

Type I medium humidity incubator with electronic thermostat and digital thermometer.

inspection facility. The incubator is constructed from 15mm chipboard a material with excellent insulating properties. A transparent secondary lid is fitted to allow examination without heat loss; for this, 'Perspex' rather than glass is suggested. In the authors incubator a 60W industrial heating element is fixed to the base but a heating pad would be equally suitable. The eggs are placed in plastic cartons within the incubator and rest on a lattice-work of wooden bars suspended above the heater. A water tray provides some ambient humidity.

Temperature control presents more of a problem. Two main types of temperature switch or thermostat are generally available. The first type relies upon a bi-metal strip and electro-mechanical action. This sort is widely available in the form of both aquarium thermostats or central heating air-temperature thermostats. Provided one is selected which encompasses the temperature range required these may be perfectly satisfactory for general use. They do however have their disadvantages. The first is that they are rarely very accurate and temperature 'swings' or deviations of several degrees are quite possible. The other disadvantage is that should they ever fail they can 'stick' open or closed thereby causing a catastrophe.

19

For some time the author has been experimenting with entirely electronic non-mechanical thermostats. These are now fairly widely available at reasonable cost and offer much increased precision and reliability over mechanical types. Such devices should be available from specialist aquatic and exotic animal suppliers or alternatively from electronic component sources. One of the best known U.K brands is 'UNO' and their 'NOVA' electronic thermostat is particularly suitable for incubator use. This type of temperature controller is becoming increasingly popular with tropical fish hobbyists so locating a suitable unit should not be too difficult.

Using an advanced proportional electronic thermostat of the authors own design a temperature tolerance of +/- 0.25° C was maintained over a 3 month period using the incubator illustrated. Whilst this sort of precision will not be required for general purpose incubation, where experiments into embryo development times or environmental sex determination (ESD) are concerned extreme accuracy will be vital.

As a method of accurate temperature control the proportional method has few equals. Unlike on-off controllers (whether mechanical or electronic) there is no time-lag whilst heating elements warm up from cold and consequently much less chance of thermal 'overshoot'. A time period (generally 10 seconds or so) is defined during which power is applied to the heating load for a variable percentage of the 'proportional band'. This percentage is determined by reference to an integrated circuit which measures deviation from the set point and either increases or decreases the percentage of 'Power On' time accordingly. The heating element itself remains warm, varying in temperature according to the percentage of time power is applied throughout the proportional band. There is no sudden surge of heat which has the additional benefit of reducing the likelihood of thermal shock damage to the element – a primary cause of failure in 'on-off' type systems.

Type II Incubator design

Where a high humidity level is required throughout incubation then the incubator shown on page 21 is recommended. Because of the humidity levels attained in this system glass or polycarbonate is the preferred constructional material and it will generally be found best to adapt a suitably sized tropical fish aquaria or plastic storage box to the purpose.

The heating element is a 75–150W submersible aquaria combined heater-thermostat. Provided that a very high quality unit is employed preferably based upon a magnetic rather than simple bi-metal switch, high levels of accuracy will be achieved. The author has used a unit manufactured by "Visitherm" which is not only constructed to a high standard but also includes a visual indication of temperature. This is

Type II high humidity incubator with submersible heater-thermostat and digital thermometer. In use a transparent plastic lid or small upturned aquarium tank is fitted over the unit.

cross-checked occasionally using a separate hand-held digital thermometer.

On many occasions I have adapted the styrofoam or polystryrene cartons tropical fish are sometimes packed in to form very functional and low-cost incubators; where only a very few eggs are to be incubated these can make an ideal base for conversion. The inside can be lined with plywood or even glass sheeting, and a heat pad can provide the heat source.

Although equally as important as temperature control temperature measurement is often overlooked – in fact there is little point in adjusting highly accurate thermostats on the basis of incorrect readings from unreliable thermometers. Experiments with alcohol and mercury thermometers revealed that low cost types were almost invariably inaccurate. If such thermometers are to be used, then those supplied for photographic processing use are often the most satisfactory.

The microchip has, however recently provided another option in the form of low cost and very satisfactory self-contained Liquid Crystal Digital (LCD) temperature modules which operate from 1.5v miniature batteries. Such units are now available at relatively low cost compared to a few years ago when they were exclusively in the domain of the laboratory and industrial user. The modules used by the author provide a LCD display of either °C or °F and are accurate to 0.1° C in most cases. In addition some models can be set to sound an audible alarm at certain temperatures – a very useful facility indeed where heater or thermostat failure can have such catastrophic consequences.

It can sometimes be useful to know the degree of variation both above and below the 'target' temperature set during any given period; for example if a batch of eggs are incubated at 31.5° C it would be very advantageous to know if overnight this temperature was actually maintained or if it suffered a fall. Such a measurement can be taken with a Maximum-Minimum recording thermometer and both mercury/alcohol and electronic versions are available. I much prefer electronic Max-Min types as these do not require physical removal to re-set (most mercury types have to be vigorously 'shaken down' after each reading has been taken). With electronic models everything can be carried out remotely by means of a switch positioned outside the incubator thereby avoiding the need to disturb the unit unnecessarily.

Humidity control has unfortunately not yet attained quite the level of sophistication of temperature control; at least not at realistic prices. The easiest way to control incident humidity within the incubator is therefore to position a tray of water in the base and to remember to re-fill it from time to time. Very accurate electronic relative humidity meters and controllers are available but are at present comparatively expensive. Whilst this may be justified in the case of research activities for day-to-day incubation purposes they are hardly essential.

It is recommended that the eggs be placed in an open topped plastic 'lunch box' within the incubator and that 'Vermiculite' or a similar insulating particle medium should be used instead of sand. Other suitable alternatives include polystyrene packaging material or agricultural potting medium – the latter is especially suitable where high humidity levels are required. 'Vermiculite' is preferred however for 'dry' incubation as it is extremely easy to sterilize and has very good thermal cushioning properties. Sand which is perhaps the most obvious choice should definitely be avoided as it can set very hard indeed during the prolonged incubation period and can entomb emerging hatchlings. It is also extremely dangerous if ingested and its well known abrasive qualities can all too easily cause serious damage to delicate eyes or mouths.

As the time for hatching approaches the open top of the incubating box can be carefully covered with coarse linen gauze or netting. Otherwise unexpected hatchlings might escape within the incubator and injure themselves.

Incubation period, temperature & ESD

Incubation time is determined not only by species but also by temperature. The higher the temperature the faster development occurs. Very high temperatures however can lead to deformity and death so it is vital to establish acceptable ranges for each species of egg it is intended to incubate. As a guide, the normal parameters for the eggs of *T. hermanni* are as follows:

<26° C = Incubation normally ineffective.

26° C – 29.5° C = All male offspring within 75–140 days.

30° C – 31.5° C = Typically mixed offspring.

32° C – 34° C = All female offspring within 60–75 days.

>34° C = Deformed hatchlings likely.

Note that this also introduces the effects of ESD, or Invironmental Sex Determination. Whilst ESD parameters have now been established for some common species, at the time of writing many species have not been investigated at all in this respect. Much field and laboratory work is crying out to be done in this fascinating and potentially highly rewarding area which has very profound implications for the conservation of endangered species of reptiles worldwide.

In the case of tortoises, terrapins and turtles low temperatures typically produce male offspring, whilst higher temperatures usually produce females. This is in marked contrast to certain other reptiles where sex is determined by temperature, particularly alligators and some lizards where the reverse is true. In the case of terrestrial chelonia, the practical relevance of all this is that even when dealing with a species where precise details of critical ESD points are unknown, the best general advice which can be offered is to incubate at between 30° C – 31° C. In most cases this should result in a mixed-sex brood which is often the most desirable objective. Incidentally, most books and articles available to the would-be captive breeder suggest incubation temperatures which are far too low, often in the 22° C – 27° C range.

Handling tortoise eggs

The effects of handling upon reptile eggs is also an area where all is by no means clear; the indications are that gentle handling following laying should not have any deleterious effect but that rough handling should definitely be avoided after embryonic development is advanced where any physical trauma could damage delicate blood vessels.

It is actually nothing more than a myth that eggs must be transported to the incubator the same way up as they were deposited in the nest. At this stage the egg contains no more than a few activated cells and these are in no way affected by orientation. Later, after an embryo has formed, orientation becomes increasingly important so after the first few days eggs should not be inverted or otherwise handled unnecessarily.

Examination of eggs during incubation

It is often possible to determine whether or not incubating eggs are fertile by carefully examining them against a strong light source. A small box, containing a 15W bulb with a hole cut in the top to hold the egg is ideal for this purpose. When subject to transillumination in this way, an egg can be examined at various stages of its development.

Such examination can usually reveal entirely infertile eggs quite easily, and those containing large embryos are also quite easy to detect; however it is not always possible to be 100% certain in borderline cases. I would certainly be very reluctant to discard any egg merely on the basis of a visual examination unless the evidence was absolutely conclusive. The only really reliable test of viability is that of time – in the final outcome eggs either hatch or they don't!

One very useful visual check which can be carried out without physically disturbing the eggs is to note any colour change; fertile eggs usually darken and gradually lose the pinkish hue of fresh laid examples. Their surface texture also becomes less reflective and somewhat less smooth to the touch – this is due to elements such as calcium being gradually lost from the shell as embryonic development continues. In infertile eggs, the composition of the eggshell remains unchanged.

Eggs can be trans-illuminated to test viability during incubation. This egg is infertile and the yolk has settled to the bottom.

Chapter Four

Hatching and the juvenile terrarium

An indication as to what actually initiates the hatching process was given earlier when the oxygen metabolism of the tortoise embryo was discussed.

As the embryo increases in size its metabolism produces an increasing quantity of carbon dioxide; eventually, this rises to a level in excess of that which can be diffused via the allantois and the pores in the eggshell (the gradual utilisation of calcium from the eggshell actually increases this porosity and gradually weakens the shell as development continues). Eventually the embryos blood and tissue CO_2 levels rise to such an extent that the embryo begins to convulse in an effort to breath normally; the head moves into the airspace within the egg created by evaporation, and lung breathing begins. This airspace rapidly becomes foul however and even stronger contractions and convulsions commence. The shape of an egg dictates that it resists compression but has little tensile strength; only slight pressure from within is sufficient to fracture it.

Some time ago, I was discussing the breeding behaviour of *Geochelone (Asterochelys) yniphora*, the extremely rare and endangered Madagascar Ploughshare tortoise, with Don Reid who has worked extensively with this species in the wild and who is achieving some notable captive breeding successes. Don disclosed that hatching usually coincided with the first heavy rains of the season. Although proof is lacking, my own feeling was that as the ground became saturated with water, permeability to oxygen would decrease sharply, the blood CO_2 levels of the hatchlings would rise and that this was quite possibly the mysterious mechanism which the young tortoises used to synchronise hatching.

Since then, I have conducted a few experiments in our own incubators. I observed that if, towards the expected hatching time, the air humidity level in the incubator was raised sharply this would tend to result in a much greater proportion of eggs hatching simultaneously than if the air

25

humidity was not raised. More research in this area might produce some interesting information.

The phenomenon of bimodality in tortoise and turtle hatching times has been noted but is not by any means well understood.

Bimodality in the context of hatching is defined as eggs from the same clutch, incubated under identical conditions, but which actually hatch at different times. It is well known that marine turtle eggs typically hatch over a very short period and that the young tend to leave the nest together. However, in tortoise eggs, it has been noted that often the time between the first hatching and the last within a clutch can be very extended. Examples include *Geochelone (Asterochelys) radiata* where one egg hatched after 121 days but another from the same clutch took 211 days to emerge, and *Geochelone pardalis* where quite frequently it can take 3-4 weeks for a clutch to complete hatching. In both *Testudo ibera* and *T. hermanni* a delay between the first and last emergence from a clutch of between 7-12 days is not at all uncommon. Even longer delays are not unheard of.

The biological reasons for this effect remain unclear; however, in one experiment I carefully monitored the incubation temperature differential between several eggs all from the same clutch which I incubated artificially using a precision incubator. At no time did the eggs differ in temperature from one another by more than 0.3° C throughout the entire incubation process. However, periodic examination of the eggs (by transillumination) revealed startling differences in the race of embryonic development, the most extreme example being that of one egg which attained hatching proportions whilst its nearest neighbour remained less than half its size. For some reason or another it appears that on occasions embryonic development is temporarily arrested in individual eggs within a clutch. There is clearly a biochemical mechanism at work here which requires further investigation.

The crucial lesson for captive breeders is not to expect all eggs to hatch 'on time' and under no circumstances to make the (usually fatal) mistake of artificially cracking open what are assumed to be 'late' eggs.

As the hatching process begins, hatchlings first abrade and then pierce the eggshell using an egg tooth like appendage (it is actually an egg-caruncle) gradually enlarging this opening by biting small pieces from the eggshell and pushing with the front legs.

Immediately hatching begins the eggs should be kept under continuous observation. Hatching can take some time; between 2-5 hours is average for *T. graeca* and *T. hermanni*. Often once access to air has been gained, the young tortoise will often stay in the egg for a day or more gradually gaining in strength and allowing time for the egg-sac to be properly

Immediately after hatching the juveniles plastron is soft and folded; it straightens out within a few days.

absorbed. If a hatchling is in obvious trouble and is clearly weakening then careful assistance can be given. Provided that hatching is in full progress giving such aid will not do any harm. If the eggshell appears to be unusually thick and is causing real problems then assistance is recommended. This can occur if the eggs have been retained in the female for a longer than usual period – indeed, on occasions twin-walled eggs are found. Such eggs are extremely hard and very likely to cause an emerging hatchling serious trouble. Usually however the walls in such cases are so thick that mortality from anoxia would have occurred long before full development has been attained.

Unless hatching has commenced naturally and it is quite clear that the time for emergence is at hand the eggs should not be otherwise disturbed. Under no circumstances should eggs be artificially cracked open on the supposition that they are "late" and hence must be in difficulty. This type of action, which is often initiated by inexpert and impatient keepers can only result in tragedy with half formed and dying hatchlings being suddenly being torn from their eggs.

Immediately hatching is complete each young tortoise as it emerges should be removed from the incubator into a previously prepared hatching vivarium or nursery unit. The now vacant eggshells should also be removed to the hatchling unit as these provide an excellent source of calcium in the critical early days and many hatchlings will avidly gnaw at them – failure to provide access to the eggshells (often discarded as of no value by many keepers!) can result in early stage calcium deficiencies. As will be seen from Table 3, in the first month the percentage growth and weight gain of hatchlings is very considerable. The calcium demand during this time is equally considerable and deficiencies can easily occur. At this point in the hatchlings life the balance between the calcium-mineral metabolism and protein metabolism is extremely fragile:- inadequate levels of dietary minerals, or excessive quantities of dietary protein will very rapidly result in the initiation of early stage osteodystrophy leading to the later manifestation of "soft-shell" syndrome and the carapace deformities so often observed in captive bred chelonians.

Initially the hatchling unit should be maintained at approximately the same temperature as the incubator. Within a few hours the environment should be adjusted to that normal for adults of the species.

The newly emerged tortoises may still have the yolk-sac attached to their plastrons. Under no circumstances should this be interfered with or any attempt made to remove it. The yolk-sac will be gradually absorbed over the next few days. Whilst it is present it represents a risk of infection so any hatchlings displaying a residual yolk-sac must be kept under the most rigorous conditions of hygiene. Sometimes yolk-sacs can adhere to the floor of the vivarium. This can be quite dangerous and steps should be taken to prevent it. One effective method is to line the hatchlings vivarium floor with polythene sheeting. A thin smear of 'KY' non-toxic jelly on the yolk-sac and on the floor can also help.

Some hatchlings may begin to drink, or feed, almost immediately; others, particulary those with yolk-sacs attached may take longer. We generally find all hatchlings are eating well within 24–48 hours, even those bearing yolk-sacs.

The environment under which captive tortoises are maintained has an absolutely critical effect upon their basic well-being and survival. Provision of an adequate and suitable environment must therefore be regarded as a major priority for all keepers.

Just occasionally deformed hatchlings or even twins may emerge from the egg – siamese twins have also been recorded. There is little to be gained from attempting to maintain grossly deformed hatchlings and should these occur it is better that they are painlessly destroyed as soon as possible. Siamese twins can sometimes be separated and the author has encountered one instance of a small parasitic embryo which was attached to a fully developed twin with which it was sharing the same egg. This was carefully separated and whilst the under-developed parasitic twin died within a few minutes its sibling survived apparently none the worse for the experience.

Table 3

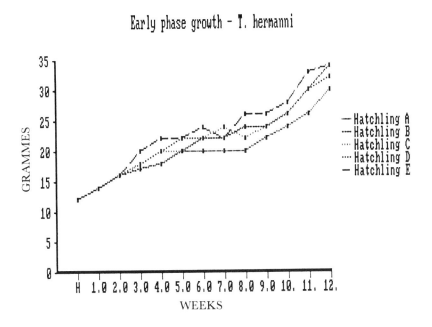

Early phase growth - T. hermanni

Legend:
- — Hatchling A
- — Hatchling B
- ··· Hatchling C
- ··· Hatchling D
- — Hatchling E

(X axis: WEEKS — H 1.0 2.0 3.0 4.0 5.0 6.0 7.0 8.0 9.0 10. 11. 12.)
(Y axis: GRAMMES — 0 5 10 15 20 25 30 35)

Although only a fraction of the size of adults, juveniles have exactly the same environmental and dietary requirements (*T. h. boettgeri* at 12 months).

29

Immediate post-hatching care

In captivity as in the wild, this is the time when young tortoises are at their most vulnerable. In the wild predation is the major cause of mortality; in captivity, poor dietary management, inadequate housing and lack of attention to disease control are among the most common reasons for losses.

Hygiene

For small hatchlings glass aquarium tanks are ideal, although be sure to allow for adequate levels of ventilation. Our own juvenile accommodation consists of aluminium and glass converted agricultural frames although for the first few weeks we use standard vivaria. The environmental requirement of hatchlings is absolutely identical to that of adults of the species.

Substrates

Provided egg-sacs have been absorbed newspaper or paper towels make

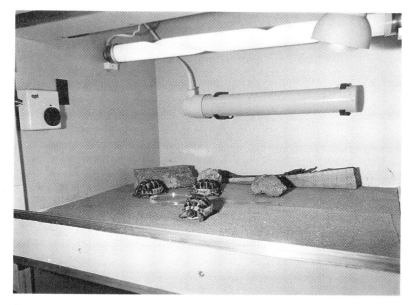

Suitable indoor hatchling vivarium with overnight tubular heater, spot lamp for basking and 'True-lite' FSL tube.

good substrates for the first few days of life. They should be changed regularly. Sand should be avoided for the reasons stated previously. Another good substrate suitable for use with hatchling tortoises can be made from alfalia or grass pellets of the sort frequently sold for rabbit food. This provides a firm footing, is very absorbent and is non toxic if ingested. Avoid medicated varieties.

Housing young tortoises

In fine weather, and provided a secure area can be provided there is absolutely no reason why the hatchlings of temperate species cannot immediately be accommodated outside; we regularly place hatchlings of only a few hours old in our (wire-mesh covered) outdoor units. Most keepers however will maintain hatchlings and juveniles indoors, at least initially or in the case of late-season hatchlings. This necessitates the use of artificial light and heat.

The most cost-effective and practical options open to those intending to set up a suitable vivarium for hatchlings may be outlined as follows;

Lighting

Various types and combinations of lighting unit can be employed, but the most consistently successful with tortoises and turtles is 'True-lite' or similar F.S.L with a tungsten supplementary lamp to encourage basking (the author finds 40W 'mini-spotlights' ideal for this, particularly those available in clamp fixing mobile holders). Species from high altitude or savannah habitats require much higher intensity illumination than those from lower altitudes which occupy jungle or forest habitats. Several 'True-lite' fixtures may be used together to provide higher intensities where indicated. Very high intensity ultra-violet lighting, as advocated in some reptile husbandry books should be avoided. It is not necessary and can cause severe tissue damage particularly in the eyes.

Heating

A wide variety of heat sources are available from specialist tropical fish accessory and vivarium suppliers as well as from electronics and industrial manufacturers. Certain types commend themselves immediately however as particularly well suited to tortoise housing applications. These include infra-red dull emitters and thermo-tubes.

Infra-red dull emitters. These are in many ways the ideal heat source for reptile cages. They are available in a wide range of powers from 60W to 250W and are easy to install. Most are shaped rather like spot lamps but instead of being constructed from glass are made from an opaque ceramic material. They get extremely hot in operation so must be installed and positioned with care using the special heatproof holders provided. Cables too must be of the heat resisting variety. They are an excellent source of basking heat for tortoises and are much appreciated by all vivarium inhabitants.

Thermo-tubes. These are cylindrical heaters usually rated at 60W/ft and are available in many different lengths from 2ft to 6ft. For small vivariums the 2' and 3' versions are best, larger units will require the 5' or 6' versions which are rated at 300W and 360W respectively. Thermo-tubes are extremely versatile and highly reliable. They may be used individually or in multiples for heating large reptile enclosures. Additional basking heat sources should be provided for most species – spot lamps as described above are an excellent choice.

Heat pads. Heat pads are sometimes recommended as an ideal form of heating for reptile cages. This view is not shared by the author who has encountered many behavioural problems linked to their use with tortoises. Heat pads provide very little direct radiant heat and can also seriously impair thermoregulatory behaviour in many species – particularly tortoises. They should not be relied upon as the sole heat source as they do not encourage natural basking. Some species are also prone to overheating if heat-pads are used. Heat pads can be used effectively in incubators and waterproof types are also very useful for base heating of aquatic turtle aquariums. Their other uses are somewhat limited with most tortoise species and they are definitely not recommended as the principal daytime source of heating for hatchlings.

It should be noted that the comments made earlier in respect of incubator thermostats and temperature controllers apply equally in respect of vivarium heating. Obviously this application is by no means as critical but some reliable method of controlling temperatures is certainly required. In practice ordinary on-off air temperature thermostats (central heating type) will be found more than adequate for controlling thermo-tubes and similar background sources whilst the precision of electronic controllers will be found of enormous benefit where I.R. emitters are to be employed.

Juveniles

Once past the immediate hatchling phase of development, which gradually takes between 3 to 6 months, options for housing widen considerably. Wherever possible we like to see young tortoises housed in outside terrarium areas. Converted agricultural glass 'cold-frames' are often ideal. These are available in various sizes, although the models we have installed measure approximately 3m × 2.25m × 450mm high. Our nursery units are of the same design but measure 700mm × 1.25mm × 450mm high. Alternatively suitable enclosures can readily be constructed using plywood or similar materials for the sides and 'Glodex' or 'Perspex' for the transparent roof. In good weather this can be removed and replaced with a wire-mesh guard. Some form of guard is essential as small tortoises are very easy prey for large birds or other predators such as foxes, weasels or rats.

The habitat should be as interesting as possible; provide an open area for basking, a heavily overgrown area for retreat, and a variety of rocks and native plants. Flat concrete floors are not acceptable and it is extremely important that everything possible is done to provide a varied, interesting, attractive and above all safe environment for young tortoises. Juveniles do not have any different temperature, light and humidity requirements than adults (they do after all hatch into the same environment as adults in the wild). Provided they are protected from predators and accidental injury they should therefore be treated identically.

Chapter Five

Natural biotype and environmental maintenance in captivity

It is extremely important when designing or installing any vivarium lighting or heating system to understand the biological implications for the animals concerned. Tortoises and turtles are reptiles and as such they are largely dependent upon their environment for adjustment and maintenance of body temperature (poikilotherms or exotherms). They have only a very limited ability to compensate for environmental temperatures either above or below their preferred optimum (P.O) level. Outside the P.O temperature, normal metabolic activity will be impaired and at excessively low or high temperatures death will occur. Unfortunately these figures are not known in detail for every species of reptile but almost all reptiles have a P.O temperature range between 20° C – 35° C, and with terrestrial chelonia the range is usually between 22° – 30° C. This is certainly a good starting range even when dealing with an 'unknown' species. Mesic species almost always have a somewhat higher P.O temperature than those species which dwell in lush jungle or undergrowth. The latter are also inclined to display poor thermoregulatory abilities.

The term 'Preferred Optimum' is in itself somewhat misleading however, and there are some indications that just because a particular temperature range may be favoured by self-selection this is not necessarily the temperature most conducive to long-term health or survival. For example, many tortoises will (if allowed to) bask under a heater all day. This can have quite serious metabolic side-effects.

So, although the 'P.O' temperature should be taken as a general guide, it should not necessarily be available at all times. Temperatures in the wild are cyclic, peaking at about mid-day and falling off towards evening. By far the best guide to ideal captive maintenance conditions will be gained from a careful study of the species natural habitat and prevailing climate. Ordinary tourist guide-books dealing with the region inhabited by the species are often a very useful source of climatic, seasonal and habitat data incidentally.

Humidity control in captive environments

The second main factor in the success or failure of the captive environment after temperature is humidity; and the importance of this should never be underestimated. Poor humidity control quite probably kills more captive tortoises than any other single environmental influence.

Humidity control can however present a real problem and unfortunately it is not possible to suggest any universal answer. In large installations de-humidifiers can help for arid habitats, and mist sprayers can be very effective in keeping things moist. Smaller installations are more difficult due to cost limitations. We have experimented for some years and so far we have found that substrates are the easiest and cheapest way to provide a fair degree of control. For arid habitat species, pebbles and rocks are suggested, and for rainforest species a combination of pine-bark mulch, peat and moss appears to work best. This latter will need changing regularly, but stones and rocks can be washed and re-used.

The three main habitat types may be summarised briefly as follows:

Mesic & arid habitats Rocky substrate, humidity low. Good air circulation essential as all mesic species prone to respiratory problems if humidity is excessive or when 'static' air conditions prevail. Direct radiant heat essential, with good gradient (usually at least 10°C between hottest and coolest part of habitat). Typically 32°C max directly under a 'spot' basking source and 20°C daytime in cool areas. Overnight, 15°C. For heat a combination of tubular heaters for background and overnight heating, plus long-wave infra-red (e.g, Dull-emitter ceramic elements) is difficult to better. This arrangement provides excellent thermoregulatory facilities (which is essential for all mesic species) and will prevent immune system depression and consequent disease problems. The lighting is also important. For the best possible environment, 'True-lite' is highly recommended. Both photo-period (daylength) and intensity of luminescence are obviously also important, but naturally vary according to the species being maintained. Time switches can certainly prove useful in setting photo-periods based upon geographical data and where tungsten lighting is used dimmer switches can also give a useful degree of control and enable 'artificial sunsets' or 'dawn-dusk' situations to be replicated.

In large vivaria or indoor habitat areas, several 'True-lite' tubes may be necessary. Certainly for some species very high light intensities are essential. I would suggest a minimum of 4 or 5 40W tubes per vivarium, or even consider using metal halide lighting systems – despite the cost. As indicated previously, good ventilation is essential (but avoid cold draughts) – small 120mm ex-computer cooling fans can be readily adapted to this application.

Many species may require burrows for retreat – and in some cases these must be at specific temperatures or humidity levels if problems are to be avoided.

Medium humidity temperate habitats This category includes all North African tortoises and most Mediterranean species. The basic requirement is for lush undergrowth, good thermoregulatory facilities, a moderate to high level of ambient humidity and good ventilation. Lighting levels should be high, with 'True-lite' highly recommended for indoor installations. For Mediterranean species several fittings may be necessary to produce the required level of illumination.

Outdoor accommodation for these species is preferable to indoor vivarium systems; *Testudo graeca, T. ibera, F. whitei, T. marginata* and *T.*

Outdoor terrarium for tropical and sub-tropical species (*Geochelone pardalis*).

hermanni all have similar requirements although *T. hermanni* and *T. ibera* can tolerate low humidity to a much greater extent than can the North African species. In very hot dry weather these species may require spraying regularly with water from a sprinkler system or hose-pipe. Pneumonia or 'runny nose syndrome' can result from inadequate levels of ambient humidity and from poor ventilation.

A secure, well protected garden area is ideal and this should include an area of open grass for basking, an area of shrubs and bushes to provide shade, a raised rocky area for climbing, and a thickly planted 'weed' area for browsing and retreat. Overnight accommodation can consist of plywood huts or houses.

Keeping tortoises out of doors without artificial support has to a certain extent gained a poor reputation as this is usually done badly, by unskilled keepers in unsuitable areas. In fact, if planned and put into practice carefully it offers enormous advantages over indoor accommodation; obviously, it is only possible with temperate species and only in areas which approximate the natural bioclimatic range of the species concerned. Fortunately, most of Europe and the U.S is within the safe range for the species mentioned above.

Certainly wherever possible I prefer to see temperate species tortoises maintained out of doors in spacious, well plated enclosures with plenty of natural cover and graze. This method of captive maintenance is vastly superior to any indoor habitat, no matter how carefully designed. For non-temperate species however, there is often no alternative to a largely indoor environment and these present special difficulties.

Rainforest and jungle habitats: Rainforest inhabitants require very different facilities and conditions from temperate species. High light intensities are rarely appreciated and can lead to severe stress. Basking heat sources are similarly not favoured. Humidity should be moderately high to very high depending upon the species. Water must be constantly available, not only for drinking, but because many of these species require a bathing pool in which they can semi-immerse themselves for hours on end and which seems to be necessary to defecation. The absence of a bathing pool will lead to serious eye inflammation, respiratory problems and dehydration. Heating is best provided by means of thermostat controlled tubular heaters of sufficient power to heat the entire vivarium to a more or less constant 25° C – 28° C (the precise setting will depend upon the species). Infra-red basking heaters are not normally required, although some specimens may take occasional advantage if one is present (e.g *Kinixys belliana* and *Geochelone (Chelonoidis) carbonaria*). In any case, a low power version is adequate (60/100W). The temperature gradient should be slight, and not more than +/- 3° C in most cases. Excessive overnight temperature variations should not occur. Lighting should not be excessively bright, and a lower power 'True-lite' fitting is usually adequate (e.g 40W). Plenty of cover should be provided as most rainforest type tortoises like to be damp, warm and well hidden.

Terrarium construction

The construction of terrariums suitable for tortoises presents considerably more difficulty than is encountered when designing similar units for smaller animals such as lizards or snakes. Without exception tortoises require sufficient space for exercise and this can obviously be a difficult criteria to meet in many indoor situations.

Rather than 'fishtank' type vivaria, which are almost never satisfactory, save for very small specimens, the only viable options for tortoises are likely to consist of converted garages, spare rooms or – best of all – converted greenhouses. Fortunately, in many countries, the maintenance of temperate species may not require much in the way of indoor accommodation at all. If tropical species are to be maintained, then an agricultural merchants building catalogue is probably a good place to seek out suitable raw materials which (with ingenuity and effort) can be often converted into first-rate terrariums.

Hibernation of temperate species

Hibernation is a complex biological process. It is also not as easy as may be thought to generalise about which species can and cannot hibernate. Certainly in the wild, some species hibernate in parts of their range and remain active throughout the winter in others. Of such species, it can best be said that they have the biological capacity to hibernate rather than to insist that they always do hibernate. Most tortoises from north Africa fall into this category.

The basic conditions for a safe hibernation may be summarised as follows;

✳ The temperature should remain above 2-3° C and below 10° C throughout the hibernation period.

✳ Animals should not be hibernated whilst their stomachs contain undigested food. A fasting period of several weeks beforehand is therefore essential.

✳ No animal which is sick or underweight should ever be hibernated.

✳ Animals should be checked frequently during hibernation. This will not harm them and it is no more than a myth that disturbing a hibernating tortoise is dangerous.

✳ Small specimens should receive only a short hibernation – 4–8 weeks is usually within safe tolerances. Even large specimens should not be subject to excessively long hibernation periods; 12–14 weeks is a typical safe maximum.

If it should become necessary to overwinter a normally hibernating temperate species, an indoor vivarium or penned area provided with heat and light as described previously will suffice.

Finally, although it is sometimes claimed that persistent non-hibernating of captive species which would naturally hibernate in the wild causes no health problems this is not an opinion we share. We have noted an increased incidence of liver disease in long-term overwintered specimens and a definite decline in fertility. We prefer to see healthy specimens hibernated and only sick or underweight specimens overwintered. As stated above, provided sufficient care is taken hibernation is not a particularly dangerous activity. The Tortoise Trust publishes a regularly up-dated guide to safe hibernation techniques which should be consulted for more detailed information on this topic.

Chapter Six

Diet & nutritional disorders

It is a fact that with very few exceptions indeed most terrestrial tortoises are exclusively herbivorous. That this is indeed the case is well borne out by physiological studies which show that the tortoises digestive system is very closely related to that of other recognised herbivores and has very little at all in common with the digestive systems of true carnivores such as snakes, cats and dogs. Biological carnivores have a rapid digestive metabolism designed for breaking down decaying animal proteins as quickly as possible and expelling the residue before toxic material can accumulate. In order to accomplish this they have short digestive tracts. Herbivores have a slow digestive metabolism better suited to steadily breaking down cellulose by gentle bacterial action. Many herbivores including cows and tortoises also make use of a retort like organ known as the caecum which functions as a kind of vat wherein vegetable cellulose is gradually fermented in addition to pancreatic based digestion. It is worth noting also that the pancreas itself is much smaller in herbivorous chelonians than it is in omnivorous or carnivorous species. Radiological studies on the alimentary tract of chelonians have revealed some quite interesting data; specifically that many weeks may be taken for food to pass completely through the gastrointestinal tract of herbivorous chelonians.

High incidences of renal and hepatic disease have been noted for some time both in veterinary reports and autopsy surveys of long-term captive chelonians. It is notable that in almost all surveys gastro-intestinal disorders are particularly significant (with parasites accounting for some, but not all of these) and that the incidence of hepatic and renal disease is much higher in animals which have been maintained principally as pets. It is interesting to note that captive herbivorous iguanas often display almost identical nutritional disorders.

40

With very few exceptions, most terrestrial tortoises are exclusively grazing herbivores.

The whole question of the provision of animal protein in the diet of captive chelonians is a contentious issue. It is sometimes argued that this is appropriate in all cases or is certainly harmless even if admittedly unnatural. The present author takes the view that animal protein is properly only appropriate to carnivorous and omnivorous species and that it is positively harmful if provided to herbivores. As noted above there are quite distinct physiological differences between these categories of animal. There are also biochemical differences which are relevant.

Uric acid and blood urea levels are greatly elevated in herbivorous chelonians fed unnatural meat based diets. Sodium urate (a salt of uric acid) which is the end result of purine metabolism is found in large quantities in meat products. Tortoises suffering from dehydration are at particularly high risk if placed on high protein animal foods as are hatchlings. It is a common (and often fatal) mistake when confronted by a dehydrated and underweight tortoise to believe that increasing the protein content of voluntary or force feeds is the best way to restore health. In fact due to the increased level of blood urea high protein foods generate renal failure is a much more likely end result.

The saturated fat content of tinned pet foods (which are the source of animal protein most frequently relied upon by tortoise keepers) is also extremely high whereas wild herbivorous chelonians would be expected to consume virtually nil saturated fat. Dried cat or dog foods in pellet form are not generally as high in fats as tinned varieties but are still far too high to be safe for consumption by tortoises.

Vitamin-A deficiency

Vitamin A is essential to healthy growth and development and in particular to epithelial condition. Deficiencies often manifest as metaplasia of the conjunctival epithelium (resulting in swollen eyes) progressing to metaplasia of the pancreatic ducts and squamous metaplasia of the renal tubules (resulting in 'blockages' of the kidneys). The external surfaces of

Proprietary vitamin and mineral supplements are very useful aids in maintaining an adequate diet in captivity.

the skin may also be raw and frequently secondary bacterial infections may also be present. There is also good reason to believe that epithelial degeneration of the lung tissues may result in respiratory problems developing and similar degeneration of the linings of the nares is certainly implicated in the aetiology of 'RNS' or Runny Nose Syndrome. Should breeding females become deficient avitaminosis-A of the egg yolk might occur; it is believed that in turn this may cause abnormal development of embryos.

Treatment consists of careful topical cleansing of external damaged areas to defeat or prevent secondary bacterial infection and provision of vitamin-A either orally or by injection in severe cases (20,000 I.u/kg). Oral dosing is best accomplished using ABIDEC or similar multi-vitamin drops. The condition can be entirely prevented if adequate levels of the vitamin are present in the diet.

Good natural (secondary) sources of vitamin-A include all fruits and vegetables containing carotene. The carotene is then converted into true vitamin-A internally. Vitamin-A and vitamins D3 and E can be overdosed (hypervitaminosis-A) so take care when administering pure doses. Secondary sources cannot be overdosed as the excess is simply not converted. 'Vionate' contains 220,000 IU per kilo and at normal levels of supplementation provides sufficient levels to prevent hypovitaminosis-A occurring. Hypervitaminosis-A or vitamin-A overdoses manifest in a manner remarkably similar to the way in which deficiencies develop with hyperkeratosis and epidermal disruption. For this reason continuous dosing with liquid vitamin drops is not recommended. The relatively low doses provided by 'Vionate' when used as recommended are within safe tolerances. One of the best natural sources is dandelion greens which contain over 14,000 i.u of vitamin-A per 100g in addition to many other vital trace elements.

Vitamin-B deficiency

Rarely encountered in terrestrial tortoises but known to present a problem in snakes and some turtles which have been fed on large quantities of frozen fish due to the presence of the enzyme thiaminase. Fish is categorically not an appropriate dietary component for terrestrial tortoises under any circumstances.

Vitamin-D3 deficiency

This condition is frequently encountered in conjunction with secondary nutritional osteo-dystrophy (see under 'Calcium'). A suitable multi-vitamin containing 15,000 IU D3 per kilo and dosed at approximately 4% weight to food will prevent the problem. The use of 'True-Lite' or similar

Gross deformity as a result of a diet too high in protein and deficient in calcium and vitamin D3.

FSL fluorescent tubes also aids natural vitamin-D utilization.

Along with vitamin-A and vitamin-E hypervitaminosis-D (i.e. over-dosing) is also a possibility which should it occur results in metastatic mineralisation of the soft tissues. Pure vitamin-D should therefore not be administered (except in cases of specific deficiency syndrome). The use of multi-vitamin products which include D3 in balanced amounts is not dangerous and will not result in excessive doses being absorbed provided they are used as directed.

Vitamin C

Vitamin C deficiency may be implicated in many conditions, especially stomatitis and a generalised susceptibility to bacterial infection. It is easily combatted by good dietary management.

Iodine deficiency

Can result from two causes; either simple lack of iodine in the diet or from the practice of feeding too many goitrogenic vegetables (typically cabbage, kale and sprouts etc). Symptoms include lethargy, fibrous goitre and myxoedema of the subcutaneous tissues. Preventative treatment consists of adequate provision of iodine in the form of vitamin-mineral preparations containing at least 30mg/kg (75mg/kg is preferable) as a trace element. Serious cases can sometimes be helped by administering sodium iodide either orally or via injection. The problem can be encountered also in wild populations especially where water supplies are naturally low in iodine.

Dietary calcium & tortoises

By far the most common nutritional disorder encountered and a major cause of early mortality in captive-bred hatchlings. This condition is sometimes known as 'soft-shell syndrome'. It is more properly called nutritional secondary osteodystrophy.

The overall body shape may also be distorted with marked elongation observed in many cases. The bones of the jaw may be soft and weak and in hatchlings the plastron may remain soft long after it ought to have hardened. These symptoms may appear collectively or individually depending upon the progression and severity of the deficiency. Hatchlings are worse affected (due to their rapid growth and consequent higher calcium demand) but even adults will manifest the condition if placed on an acutely deficient or severely unbalanced diet for long enough during a growth phase. The condition results directly from inadequate levels of

Excessive dietary protein causes unnaturally accelerated growth and deformed, raised scutes. This specimen is only two years old and is over 200% larger than is natural at that age.

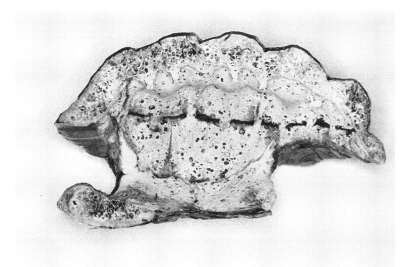

Acute osteo-porosis, with thickened, porous boney tissue and raised scutes. This tortoise was raised on a diet of tinned dog food. It died of renal failure and severe calcium deficiency.

dietary calcium, excessive dietary protein and inadequate levels of vitamin D3. Generally a combination of factors are involved.

Tortoises fed on a lettuce only (or almost) diet without mineral supplementation will suffer from classic softshell syndrome. Those fed on high protein diets combined with a relative calcium deficiency will suffer from acute softshell syndrome plus gross 'pyramiding' of the scutes and excessively high blood urea levels. Such animals may well go on to develop serious renal damage and other diseases associated with uric acid deposition.

The ideal ratio of calcium to phosphorous in herbivorous species is often quoted 2:1 for growing reptiles, at least 1.25:1 for fully grown adults, and 15 or even 20:1 in the case of carnivorous species. Calculations based upon the chemical constituents of wild tortoise diets suggest that an actual figure of 4 or even 6 parts calcium to 1 part phosphate would be more realistic. 'Vionate' is an excellent supplement which contains many valuable trace elements and vitamins. It is not however sufficiently rich in calcium to counterbalance the high phosphate levels encountered in many green vegetables. Even where it is provided liberally it is very difficult to maintain a ratio of 1:1 or 2:1 in practice and virtually impossible to exceed these levels. One answer is to supplement with additional raw calcium lactate, and in this way a true working ratio of between 4 to 6:1 is fairly readily achieved.

At the same time it is important that strongly negative Ca:P food items are totally excluded from the diet and all dietary constituents should be selected so that the overall dietary calcium to phosphorus ratio (prior to supplementation) is at worst neutral and if at all possible positive.

Some specialist suppliers of reptile vitamin and mineral supplements now offer products which have been carefully formulated to provide a much better match to the specific dietary requirements of reptiles than the standard supplements (such as 'Vionate') which were originally formulated for general purpose use. One such supplier in the U.K. is Vetark Products whose 'Nutrobal' high calcium supplement is especially suitable for tortoises and turtles.

Our own experience of rearing hatchlings of a variety of species both temperate and tropical, herbivorous and omnivorous, has proven beyond any doubt that this destructive condition can be entirely prevented if a balanced vitamin-mineral supplement is provided to all hatchlings and growing tortoises. Our preferred sources are 'Vionate' (Ciba-Giegy) a multi-vitamin and mineral preparation which we administer at approximately 4% of food weight daily and Vetark Products 'Nutrobal'. It is important to note that only fresh stocks which have been kept in an airtight container are satisfactory. Outdated stocks or supplies which have been kept in bags rather than sealed containers have drastically reduced effectiveness due to oxidisation of volatile vitamins. We further supplement the 'Vionate' with additional calcium to bring the Ca:P ratio to the correct level of around 5 or 6 parts calcium to 1 part phosphate. With 'Nutrobal' no such calcium additives are necessary.

It is frequently assumed that a tortoises calcium demand is relatively stable and constant; in fact this is not so. It fluctuates quite considerably and is much higher in females during egg production and in both sexes during any period of rapid growth than it is in periods of low growth or in old age. It is therefore our practice to provide all breeding females with additional sources of calcium to aid egg production.

Tortoises and turtles which consume meat have different requirements in respect of calcium than 100% herbivores. This is a very important factor which goes far beyond mere dietary preference; it actually produces changes upon a very sensitive biochemical and physiological balance. Provision of the incorrect diet will severely disrupt this balance.

Carnivorous and semi-carnivorous species are especially prone to calcium-phosphorus imbalance such animals receiving on average a ratio of 1:25 from red meat diets, or if the diet consists of meat and fish (as in the case of terrapins) 1:10 and 1:16 if mainly insect based.

Good natural sources of calcium include apricots, figs, fig leaves, dandelions, chicory and parsley. It should be noted that whilst members of the *Chenopodiacea* family (specifically spinach and beet greens) appear on the surface to offer a good source of calcium this is tied up with oxalic acid, a substance which forms insoluble calcium oxalate and is thus of limited value to the tortoise.

Dietary fibre

This is frequently overlooked but in fact is extremely critical to a tortoises well being. A lack of sufficient dietary fibre will result in poor digestion, diarrhoea and an increased risk of colic. It is also very probable that the fibrous nature of wild tortoises foods may well assist the rapid removal of intestinal parasites and that lack of fibre may be one factor in these attaining dangerously high concentrations in captive specimens.

An examination of faeces samples taken from wild tortoises reveals fibre contents many times greater than that typical in captive animals. Wild tortoise faeces are generally well compacted, well formed and very high in varied grass content. This should be compared to the loose, poorly formed droppings so often seen in captive collections.

A diet rich in fibre is therefore highly desirable and attempts should be made to ensure that adequate quantities are available. This can take many forms, but lucerne, hay and banana leaves have provied highly effective especially in the case of captive giant species. Note however that some high fibre items may be high in protein and have a negative Ca:P balance. This should be investigated and if necessary adjustments made to the overall dietary regime to compensate. One comparatively easy way to increase the dietary fibre intake is to provide dried green leaf or grass material. Hatchlings especially seem to enjoy this and it is generally consumed avidly. Where it is provided the resulting faeces is comparable to that of a healthy wild specimen.

Water and dehydration

Another extremely critical area which is often completely ignored is provision of adequate supplies of water either as drinking water or as an integral component of plant foods. The problem is again compounded if animal proteins are fed to inappropriate species.

Tortoises secrete nitrogenous waste matter as uric acid. In order to remain in solution this requires the reptile to absorb large amounts of water. If insufficient water is available the urates and uric acid precipitate out of solution and form chalky white or yellowish concretions throughout the body, mainly in the kidneys but also in other organs and even in the joints (visceral and articular gout). Uric acid is much more insoluble than urea and therefore dehydration even for very short periods of time can have extremely drastic consequences. It should never be allowed to occur under any circumstances. If dehydration is combined with a diet dangerously high in protein the result is even more catastrophic.

Tortoises emerging from hibernation and anoretic animals are at special risk as are those maintained under conditions where ready access to water is denied. Female tortoises also require additional water during egg-production. Treatment consists of rehydration preferably using specialist solutions such as compound sodium lactate (Hartmann's Solution) and various proprietary oral rehydration therapies based upon sodium, potassium, magnesium and chloride. Where renal problems already exist, 'flushing' the system with pure water or Hartmann's solution is the preferred option.

It is a common mistake of non-specialists upon encountering a severely dehydrated and probably emaciated animal to begin treatment by force feeding quantities of high protein food. This is inclined to have lethal consequences. Treat dehydration first and only when that has been effectively dealt with and renal function is entirely satisfactory move on to treat the underlying emaciation.

Acute dehydration can occur with surprising rapidity in hatchlings and small tortoises and keepers must always be on the alert for early signs. These include the absence of urination, loss of skin elasticity, sunken eyes and weight loss. Such symptoms should never be ignored and must always be dealt with urgently.

It ought to be noted that certain species, particularly *Kinixys* spp., *Geochelone (Chelonoidis) carbonaria* and others require constant access to drinking and bathing water in order to urinate or defecate normally. The absence of suitable water supplies will inhibit normal behaviour and can lead to a drastic increase in retained toxin levels and consequent renal stress.

Steatitis and dietary fat content

This is a common condition of captive pet tortoises and is a disease of excess rather than deficiency. It is found in tortoises which have been fed on high fat diets and is also widespread in turtles and terrapins fed on oily fish such as whitebait. Tortoises fed on tinned dog and cat food are most at risk.

Provision of milk and milk-based products in the diet is also a very common cause and these must never be given under any circumstances. Other highly dangerous substances sometimes fed to tortoises by misguided owners include cheese – the latter typically consisting of 35g fat and 26g protein per 100g.

The condition is characterised by obesity and by the concretion of yellowish nodules of fat throughout the thoracic cavity and invasive build-up of fat in the liver. Jaundice is a frequent consequence. Existing cases may respond to vitamin-E which has antioxidant properties as well as anabolic steroids and thyroxine. Jaundice can also be assisted by oral dosing with the amino-acid methionine (200mg every 48 hours for 5 doses in most cases) which mobilises fat stored in the liver. Adequate levels of choline in the diet together with vitamin-E supplementation can also help.

Protein requirement

The protein requirements of most reptiles have not been studied in sufficient detail, and no specific figures have so far been established for herbivorous terrestrial chelonians. Analysis of the native diet of *Xerobates (Gopherus) agassizi*, which in many respects is typical of arid habitat chelonian herbivores, suggests that the protein content of the food intake ranges from 1% (*Opuntia* Spp.) with grasses at a median protein content of 5% constituting a major part of the dietary intake. A safe upper protein content limit for items which are regularly included in the diet would

Solidified uric acid passed by *T. graeca*. High protein diets (dog food and peas, in this instance) produce high levels of urea in the blood which then which has to be excreted by the kidneys. The end result is often kidney failure.

seem to be circa 7%, as this is about as high as is ever attained in the wild by most species, even during peak periods of food availability. An average intake level of 4% would represent a close approximation of that experienced in the natural habitat.

Despite the lack of detailed information on protein demand, it is certain that the figure is very much lower Kg for Kg than mammals where 0.5g of usable protein per Kg would be a typical daily requirement. It seems probable that the daily requirement of a growing tortoise is in the approximate region of 0.20g of usable protein per Kg, although this may well vary considerably according to species and metabolic rate. Against this it should be noted that even such a low quality food item as lettuce contains on average 1g of protein per 100g, and most legumes contain well in excess of 7g/100g.

Excess dietary proteins are converted by the liver into carbohydrates and fat. The first stage is to split the protein to amino acids which are then deaminated (i.e the NH2 group is removed and converted into urea). It is via this mechanism that dangerously high blood urea levels are generated when herbivores are placed on protein rich diets resulting not only in hepatic problems but also in acute renal distress. It should be noted that meat and meat products are not the only way in which this problem can be caused, tortoises fed excessive quantities of beans and similar protein-rich vegetable matter can also suffer the same effects.

Excessive quantities of protein can also seriously impair the calcium metabolism, and in addition can lead to massively accelerated growth and early sexual maturity. This is readily observed in many captive-bred hatchlings, where 2 year old specimens raised on high protein diets frequently weigh four to five times the weight which they could reasonably expect to attain in the wild, demonstrate abnormally advanced sexual behaviour and – invariably – deformed 'pyramid-like' scutes and grossly distorted carapaces. This latter effect is even seen in cases where otherwise adequate levels of calcium and vitamin D3 have been provided. Those fed on canned animal foods also tend to display definite melanistic characteristics, with much darker than usual carapace colouring (due to excessive thickening of the layers of keratin forming the scutes). In acute cases the carapace is weak and bulging and the horny shields or scutes are raised and pyramid-like especially along the central vertebral line. Radiological examination reveals gross distortions and separation of the underlying bone as well as poor bone density.

The solution is not to provide excessive quantities of protein and to ensure that mineral-vitamin levels are carefully balanced and are available in sufficient quantities. We may summarise the ideal diet for herbivorous species as consisting of the following;

LOW in fats, oils and protein

RICH in minerals and vitamins

HIGH in fibre

ADEQUATE in water content

Try to provide as wide a range of suitable foods as possible not ignoring more unusual items provided they meet the above criteria. Avoid over reliance upon one staple foodstuff; tortoises can easily become 'addicted' to lettuce or similar items with unfortunate consequences. Be absolutely certain to add a suitable vitamin-mineral supplement.

The requirements of omnivorous and carnivorous species (principally fresh-water aquatic chelonians) are obviously somewhat different but even so try to provide an interesting and varied diet adequate in trace elements and vitamins. Be particularly careful to ensure that the calcium – phosphorous balance is maintained within safe tolerances. Tinned cat and dog foods are not the best choice for chelonians even where animal proteins may justifiably be included in the diet (e.g Box tortoises) due to their extremely high saturated fat content. Where such material is to be provided dried processed meat pellets are a much better choice. Not only are these usually already vitamin and mineral enriched with a far lower fat content than tinned foods, but their fibre content is also much higher. Their vitamin and mineral content can be further enhanced by dressing each serving liberally with 'Vionate' and calcium or 'Nutrobal'.

Suggested general feeding program

The following suggested base diet applies to *Testudo hermanni*, *Testudo graeca*, *Testudo horsfieldi*, *Furculachelys whitei*, *Testudo marginata* and most other tortoises from similar habitats – e.g, *Geochelone pardalis* (the Leopard tortoise) and *Geochelone (Chelonoidis) chilensis* (the Chaco tortoise). Exactly the same dietary profile has also been used with great success for *Geochelone (Chelonoidis) carbonaria* – the South American Red-foot tortoise.

Mixed green-lead vegetable base: Dandelion; cabbage (mixed varieties); clover shoots; kale; lettuce; parsley; carrot toppings; sowthistle; coarse mixed grasses etc.

Fruit: Melon (both red and white); tomato; mango; pineapple; cauliflower; apple; pear; red and green sweet peppers; cucumber; marrow etc.

Mix these all together in a large bowl or bucket and apply liberal quantities of 'Vionate' or other high quality multi-mineral and vitamin supplement plus some extra raw calcium.

This diet has been proven to provide more than adequate protein, fibre and trace elements even for breeding females of such large and rapidly growing species such as *Geochelone pardalis* and *Geochelone (Chelonoidis) carbonaria*. The hatchlings are also raised on this dietary regime with really excellent results – carapace growth is smooth and even with excellent bone development. Post hatching juvenile mortality is practically zero, the only losses being recorded in cases of congenital deformity. No dietary related fatalities have been noted whatsoever since this program was adapted as standard in or own collection, or in the collections of various zoos which have adopted it.

* Fruit should be used sparingly with some species – over ingestion can result in high levels of sugar in the gut which can in turn lead to a proliferation of digestive tract parasites, especially flagellates.

Chapter Seven

Parasitic diseases

Parasites present a major hazard to tortoises and turtles and if adequate preventative steps are not taken significantly increase the incidence of ill health and mortality. Early detection of parasite problems are an essential part of the duties of any responsible reptile keeper.

Parasites which affect tortoises fall into two classes ecto-parasites which are found outside the body, and endo-parasites which are found internally and include 'worms' and protozoan infections. Ecto-parasites such as mites and ticks are generally only found on new imports, animals obtained from reptile dealers premises or which have been maintained in close proximity to other animals, such as in zoos and outside enclosures. Ticks often congregate in the soft, fleshy parts around the tops of the legs, neck and tail; all newly introduced animals should be examined carefully for any evidence of their presence.

Fortunately ticks can be removed fairly easily. They can be coated with alcohol and petroleum jelly then turned on their backs in order to loosen their grip, and the mouth parts firmly prised away. Coat the resulting puncture wound with 'Betadine' or similar povidone-iodine solution. If mouth parts are allowed to remain embedded quite serious abscesses may result.

Mites are more difficult to deal with but fortunately they are not as widespread on tortoises as they are on snakes and lizards so will only very rarely be encountered. A very thorough all-over bath with 'Betadine' sometimes works but by far the best method of treatment involves low level exposure to dichlorvos, usually as 'Vapona' insecticide. It should be made clear that this substance is highly toxic and that extreme care is necessary in its use. An otherwise useful group of anti-parasitic agents called ivermectins are contra-indicated for use in tortoises as there are indications of unusually severe toxic reactions including reports of fatalities.

Flies and maggots are also a potential problem; flies because in addition to causing irritation and laying eggs on wound sites are quite capable of transmitting many other bacterial diseases and of spreading protozoan infections. Flies in the reptile house should be eliminated and any wounds where flies are likely to be attracted should be treated with antibiotic preparations which include an organophosphorus insecticide compound to destroy any larvae.

Before passing on to examine various parasites in detail it is worth pointing out that in an ideal reptile house parasite prevention would begin with the architects. Corners of cages should be smooth and easy to clean, floors non-porous, and water supplies for each cage or pen entirely independent. Ventilators should be equipped with fly traps and all cages should be completely isolated from each other. A small laboratory bench equipped with a microscope would also be a vital accessrory.

Nematodes

Helminth ('worm') infestations are by far the most commonly encountered chelonian parasite. Two major classes of helminth are involved; long, round and greyish-pink types called ascarids and small, white thread-like types called oxyurids.

Ascarid helminths of the type *Angusticaecum* as commonly isolated from mediterranean tortoises may measure up to 100mm in length but generally do not cause as much irritation and discomfort to the animal as do the smaller oxyurid species such as *Tachygonetria* and *Atractis* which typically measure less than 5mm.

Treatment is straightforward for both types of nematode and consists of introducing by stomach tube a measured quantity of an effective and safe anthelmintic. Previously drugs such as Piperazine and Phenothiazine have been suggested in various publications as has L-Tetramisole. Unfortunately it is clear that these particular drugs are not actually very effective and that Piperazine is in addition toxic to tortoises and particularly so if the specimen is debilitated or dehydrated. It should be carefully noted that as most cat and dog 'worming tablets' are in fact based upon piperazine salts they should definitely not be used. Another drug which is contra-indicated is Thiabendazole as its hydroscopic qualities can accelerate dehydration and disrupt the electrolyte balance.

The following drugs are safe in all chelonians including hatchlings and debilitated specimens (but be careful in the case of dehydrated animals; in such instances we prefer Oxfendazole). Both have the major advantage that they are ovicidal – killing the parasitic ova as well as the adult worms.

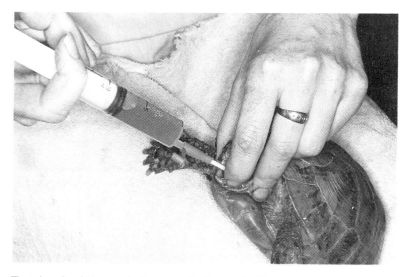

Tortoises should be regularly wormed using a suitable worming solution which is delivered via stomach tube. The same handling technique is used to deliver fluid in cases of dehydration.

FENBENDAZOLE (trade name Panacur). Suggested dose rate is 50mg per kilo repeated after 14 days.

OXFENDAZOLE (trade names Synathic or Systamex). Suggested dose rate is 65mg per kilo with no repeat dose normally necessary except in very high level infestations. This is equivalent to 3ml per kg of the standard 2.265% suspension.

Diagnosis. Microscopic examination is by far the best method of screening for helminths. A faecal sample should be collected and placed into a test tube with a quantity of saline solution (salt). This should be shaken vigorously then allowed to stand for at least an hour. Faecal debris will precipitate to the bottom of the test tube and a pipette should then be used to extract a sample from the top of the solution. This should be placed on a microscope slide (preferably of the 'well' type) and examined for both ova and immature worms.

Physical symptoms of acute helminth infestation include diarrhoea, anorexia and possible vomiting of worms. If large scale infestation is allowed to remain untreated serious perforations of the intestine leading to peritonitis or even intestinal blockages can occur. Low level infestation

55

may not be pathogenic. The ability of ascarids to enter the bile and pancreatic ducts can also result in obstructions forming which in turn can lead to hepatic necrosis and jaundice.

Cestodes and Trematodes

Cestodes (tapeworms) are extremely rare in heribvorous chelonians but may be encountered in carnivorous species and in aquatic turtles where they are relatively common. The same applies to Trematodes, or flukes.

Oxfendazole used as directed above is an effective treatment although Niclosamide at 150mg/kg has also been suggested. Dichlorophen at 180mg/kg is another useful agent. These particular parasites ought not to present too many problems as they require an intermediate host and this condition will rarely be met in captivity.

Flagellate organisms

Flagellates may present a major problem in captive collections. Symptoms include diarrhoea, passage of undigested food, dehydration and anorexia. The condition is potentially serious and should be identified as early as possible. Under the microscope many very small highly motile organisms will be observed in the fresh faecal samples.

Treatment of protozoan infection is recommended using Metronidazole. It has been found that the standard suspension (Benzoylmetronidazole) can cause vomiting in some species, particularly *T. hermanni*. Therefore it is suggested that 200mg Metronidazole tablets should be suspended in sterile water and administered by stomach tube. Several dosing schedules have been recommended from single doses at 260mg per kilo, to 160mg per kilo for 4 days, to 25mg per kilo for 10 days. Treatment with Dimetronidazole may also be effective although generally Metronidazole remains the preferred choice.

When flagellates are detected, one is faced with the problem of whether or not to initiate treatment. The obvious course – of treating regardless – is not necessarily advisable as these organisms are by no means always pathogenic. Our own approach is to obtain treatment whenever they appear to be causing a problem, and to merely monitor their presence otherwise. We have found that many tortoises seem able to tolerate their presence with absolutely no ill effects and others are able to recover very quickly without veterinary intervention from mild attacks. If it becomes obvious that the organisms are causing a persistent nuisance, then we initiate treatment with Metronidazole as described above.

One outcome of severe flagellate infections, and a problem which is compounded by the necessity of having to use Metronidazole to remove them, is a condition which we term 'Sterile Gut Syndrome', where the symbiotic gut flora are either severaly depressed or in some cases eliminated entirely. Re-establishing viable colonies of such bacteria can prove difficult. Meanwhile the affected animal is completely unable to digest food and in effect starves even though it may continue to eat. Two solutions have proved effective. In milder cases, provided some bacteria remain, symbiotic flora can often be persuaded to regenerate if either natural (live) yoghurt or a proprietary metabolic stabiliser are administered by stomach tube and the animal is kept at optimum temperatures to encourage maximum intestinal bacterial activity. In severe cases, where total sterility has occurred, a live bacterial infusion made from healthy tortoises faeces is the often the only effective answer. Should this latter course prove necessary, a sample of faeces should be obtained from another tortoise, screened carefully by microscopic examination for pathogens, liquidised, then administered in a fluid solution via stomach tube. The faeces of hatchling tortoises, should any be available, are especially suitable as these will have been maintained under conditions of maximum security from contamination by serious pathogens.

Where 'scour' or the passage of undigested food continues for more than 2 weeks following flagellate infestation, Sterile Gut Syndrome should be suspected. In the early stages most cases respond to the administration of yoghurt or metabolic stabiliser; if the condition has persisted for some time then treatment with a living bacteria native to herbivorous chelonians will almost certainly prove the most effective course.

Dietary deficiencies or excesses are a prime cause of flagellate infestation; an excessive intake of sugar-rich fruit is one particularly common factor. Another factor is an inadequate consumption of dietary fibre. Very frequently, even severe flagellate problems can be overcome if the keeper pays more attention to dietary management. Where tortoises are allowed to graze under near natural conditions, our experience is that flagellate (and nematode) problems are almost never encountered.

Finally it should be noted that where tortoises are maintained at excessively high overnight temperatures, or where unrestricted access to heat lamps is provided by daytime flagellate outbreaks are particularly commonplace; this may be due to temperature accelerated gut function. We certainly prefer to see temperate species allowed to remain cool overnight. This frequently clears the problem without additional veterinary intervention.

Hexamitiasis

A serious flagellate infection of the renal system caused by the organism *Hexamita parva*. This condition should be treated whenever it is detected as the organism concerned is highly pathogenic resulting in either acute or chronic nephritis. Symptoms include passage of strongly smelling urine (sometimes tinged green) and in severe cases flecked with blood. Other symptoms may include excessive drinking, anorexia and loss of weight. Treatment is with Metronidazole at 50mg/kg over 10 days. We have also eliminated these organisms using a single large dose of Metronidazole at 260mg/kg repeated after 2 weeks. If caught in the early stages nephritis can be prevented but if allowed to progress untreated for any length of time the prognosis is not good. Affected animals should be isolated, handled using contamination procedures and their progress carefully monitored. *Hexamita* are very small and a moderately powerful microscope will be needed in order to identify them.

Balantidiosis

A ciliate protozoan organism of doubtful pathogenicity in tortoises. It is often found in conjunction with other organisms and may simply be opportunistic. We have detected it in *T. graeca*, *T. hermanni*, *Malacochersus tornieri* and *G. pardalis*. It has also been recorded in other species. Although no specific treatment exists we have has 100% success using Metronidazole at 260mg/kg in a single dose.

Miscellaneous ciliate protozoa

Other ciliate organisms identified in tortoises include *Nyctotherus kyphodes*, and *N. teleacus* from several giant species, as well as *Geochelone (Chelonoidis) carbonaria*, *G. elegans*, *Gopherus polyphemus* and *Kinixys belliana*. Once again the pathogenicity of these organisms is not established. *Balantidium coli* causes abscessing in pigs and one of the tortoises we encountered harbouring *Balantidium testudinis* was suffering from this condition; whether or not there was a connection however remains unknown.

Amoebiasis

Not a major problem in tortoises but persons who keep other reptiles ought to recognise that the organism *Entamoeba invadens* may be carried harmlessly by chelonians. This organism is manifestly not harmless in snakes where it results in a high mortality. Never allow tortoises to mix with other reptiles, e.g snakes or lizards. The very high incidence of both parasitic and bacterial infection often seen in dealers stocks is due almost entirely to poor hygiene and random association of mutually incompatible species.

Mycoses

We have recently encountered several cases of ulcerative shell disease resulting from a fungal infection, and infections of the lungs and intestines have also been recorded. External mycoses often respond to treatment with Betadine providone-iodine solution or malachite green and a specific anti-fungal drug Nystatin is useful in cases of internal infection.

Much can be done to reduce the possibility of infections by all parasitic pathogens;
* Tortoises of different species should not be allowed to mix. Particularly, carnivorous and herbivorous species should be maintained in strict isolation.
* Keepers should pay rigorous attention to hygiene, especially regarding food handling and preparation.
* All tortoises should be checked for parasites regularly. This can easily be accomplished by placing individuals in large plastic lined isolation areas in order to be sure of collecting adequate faeces and urine samples.

The prevention and control of parasites in captive collections is often not treated as seriously as it ought to be. This is regrettable as post-mortem surveys consistently demonstrate a link between overall mortality encountered in collections and the incidence of parasitism. Parasites are not only harmful directly but indirectly as vectors for the transmission of bacterial diseases and other pathogens. Every reptile keeper should be aware of the dangers presented by parasites and should initiate regular checks and obtain immediate veterinary treatment as soon as a problem is developing in the collection.

Chapter Eight

Bacterial diseases

The subject of bacterial diseases in reptiles is a vast one and can only be discussed here briefly. Bacterial diseases are certainly one of the major causes of mortality in captive collections, as many published post mortem surveys have shown.

Most of the preventative measures suggested for counteracting parasitic contagion will also prove effective against the transmission of bacterial diseases, i.e good hygiene and careful handling. Certainly the regular use of providone-iodine disinfectants can make a considerable contribution. Other more common disinfecting agents may not be suitable including those based upon phenols where unless considerable care is exercised toxic effects may be noted. Phenols are however generally very effective against Gram-negative bacteria, and provided due caution is exercised may prove useful in some circumstances. Products based upon quaternary ammonium compounds are frequently ineffective against Gram-negative pathogens, and are therefore of extremely limited use in reptile maintenance applications where such pathogens predominate.

Necrotic Stomatitis

Until a few years ago this condition was almost invariably fatal unless observed in a very mild form. Today the vast majority of cases make a full recovery. We owe this dramatic turnaround in no small way to the development of much more effective antibiotics. Cultures taken from tortoises with 'mouth-rot' almost invariably reveal the presence of Gram-negative organisms, often *Pseudomonas* or *Aeromonas* spp. In the very early stages mild cases often respond to oral swabbing with Betadine or a similar providone-iodine solution. If the infection is well established then antibiotic therapy is vital. Therapies based upon chloramphenicol, ampicillin or tetracycline are unlikely to be successful for this condition although the oral cephalosporins have proved highly useful even in cases of aminoglycoside resistant strains. In every case, before antibiotics are actually applied, a swab should be taken for bacteriological culture. Whilst results are awaited treatment should not be delayed but should commence immediately the swab is taken using the most promising therapy under the particular circumstances.

In very severe cases where osteo-myelitis of the mouth or jaw has occurred (i.e the bone has become infected), the topical application of Framycetin or other selected agent may be usefully supplemented with

The mouth is a common site of bacterial infections. Here, infected tissue is gently cleansed prior to application of a topical antibiotic.

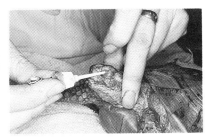

Swollen and infected eyes often respond to a topical application of antibiotic ointment.

systemic therapy at 10mg/kg every 48 hours for a full course of 5 injections. This dose ought not to be exceeded due to the renal toxicity of the aminoglycoside antibiotic. The affected area should be regularly debrided, cleansed using povidone-iodine swabs and the animal placed under intensive care support whilst undergoing therapy.

Ocular Infections

Most eye infections encountered in tortoises are comparatively easy to treat. We have observed excellent response to cloxacillin as well as to neomycin. Chloramphenicol ointment has also proved very useful. More serious infections have responded to gentamycin and tobramycin given as eye drops.

Many ocular infections begin as a small white spot on the surface of the cornea. If untreated this can rapidly spread until the entire cornea is completely obscured and ulcerated. This condition ought not to be confused with a typical cataract, which it can closely resemble. Other ocular infections involve the surrounding tissues and can cause severe local swelling and irritation. Frequently such cases are secondary to hypovitaminosis-A, especially in hatchlings or aquatic chelonians.

Cloacitis

An inflamed or ulcerated cloacal opening often combined with an unpleasant discharge often indicates the presence of cloacitis. The condition is sometimes encountered in combination with parasite infestation, or cloacal calculus (a stone-like object formed within the cloaca). If the latter is present it should be removed. Two very effective modes of treatment include irrigating the cloaca with 50% dilute Betadine (Povidone-Iodine) solution and the introduction of an antibiotic paste directly into the cloaca. Most cases respond very quickly.

Ear Abscesses

These are extremely common (especially in Box Tortoises) although we have encountered them in almost all species including *Kinixys* and *Geochelone* spp. The main symptom is a swelling of the tympanitic membrane and the discharge of pus into the back of the throat via the eustachian tube. We have noted success on a few occasions with systemic therapy, but only in the very early stages. The vast majority of cases encountered will be far too advanced for this to stand any chance of success however and surgical excision under a general anaesthetic is by far the best course of action. Recent advances in cryosurgery offer new and very promising alternatives.

Note that environmental factors and general hygiene standards are often implicated in the occurrence of this condition. In the case of American Box Turtles excessively high vivarium temperatures and inadequate humidity levels can certainly contribute to the problem.

Ulcerative Shell Disease

USD or "Shell-rot" is an unpleasant condition which can take two forms, one 'dry' the other 'wet'. The former appears to be not of bacterial origin at all, but a mycoses or fungal infection. See the notes on this earlier. The 'wet' form is caused by Gram-negative bacteria invading an existing lesion, and is typified by a fluid discharge (often foul smelling and tinged with blood) which seeps from between the scutes of the carapace. This condition requires urgent veterinary attention, as if left untreated it will almost invariably progress to generalised septicaemia.

Treatment consists of removal of affected shields and thorough cleansing with Betadine or similar povidone-iodine solution. Exposure of the affected sub-shield area to air certainly helps as most responsible organisms are anaerobic and exposure to oxygen seems to limit their ability to replicate. A topical antibiotic ointment should also be applied in advanced cases, framycetin is generally recommended. Recently we have also noted good results with 1% silver sulphadiazine in paste form and this appears to be very effective against *Pseudomonas* and other Gram-negative pathogens. This preparation is a topical antibacterial formulation originally developed for the treatment of severe burns in mammals. In very advanced cases where myelitis has occurred systemic antibiotic therapy may also be required; again the antibiotic agents of choice are framycetin, gentamycin or amikacin at the dose rates described previously.

The organisms most frequently isolated from USD in terrestrial tortoises include *Pseudomonas*, *Citrobacter*, and *Klebsiella*. Routine sensitivity tests reveal that all are frequently highly resistant to certain antibiotics and that best sensitivity is generally shown to framycetin, tobramycin and gentamycin among the aminoglycosides and to oxytetracycline among the non-aminoglycosides. One vital aspect of this which we cannot over-emphasise is the need to undertake sensitivity tests to establish exactly which organisms are present in any given case and what they are sensitive or resistant to. Treatment should not be delayed whilst tests are undertaken, but commenced using the most promising drug under the circumstances.

Septic arthritis & articular gout

A condition occasionally found in long-term captive tortoises of *T. graeca*

63

or *T. hermanni* however its incidence in the wild is unknown. To date, we have not observed the condition in other species although there is no reason to suppose it does not occur with the same frequency.

We have recently become convinced that there is a link between this condition and excesssively high intakes of dietary protein. This may cause urea to be deposited in the joints and thereby initiate the condition. Definite proof is lacking, but our data shows that the incidence of the condition is considerably higher in normally herbivorous species which have been subjected to a diet rich in animal derived proteins (e.g dog and cat food) than those which have had a more natural diet. Secondary bacterial infection of the affected joint then follows.

The main symptom is a swelling of the legs and stiffening of the joints. Some cases respond to systemic antibiotic treatment. Success has been reported using oxytetracycline, but we have had very good results with gentamycin and framycetin. If only one leg is affected it is sometimes best to amputate, particularly if tissue destruction is advanced. Where more than one leg is affected, amputation is not viable for humane reasons and reliance must be placed on drug therapy. X-rays are a very useful diagnostic tool when confronted by these symptoms as they can reveal the extent to which the joints and bones have been affected.

Abscesses

Abscesses are extremely common in all reptiles, and we have encountered them very frequently indeed in chelonians. The most common sites in order of incidence recorded are the ears, legs, nasal passages and jaw. Internally, abscesses are also often located in the liver when they are associated with clinical symptoms of acute jaundice. Abscesses often manifest in the form of hard, subcutaneous lumps and swellings. The pus they contain is usually yellow and caseous, often a fibrous capsule is present.

Treatment is best carried out by surgical excision (although new techniques in cryo-surgery once again appear highly promising); in our experience attempts to treat systemically are almost always ineffectual, save in the very small number of cases caught in the earliest stages. The entire abscess should be carefully removed (usually under a local or a general anaesthetic) and the area irrigated with antiseptics or antibiotics. Suturing may be necessary in certain instances. Often healing progresses better without suturing however, provided repeated post-operative antibacterial irrigation is undertaken.

Isolates of bacteria cultured from chelonian abscesses included mainly *Pseudomonas*, *Aeromonas* and *Citrobacter*, with *Proteus*, *Serratia*, *Enterobacter* and *Klebsiella* also present in many cases. The best antibiotic sen-

64

sitivity tended to be to the aminoglycosides gentamycin, framycetin and neomycin.

Respiratory diseases

In the authors experience the two major respiratory problems of bacterial origin associated with the captive maintenance of chelonia are pneumonia and 'R.N.S' or "runny nose syndrome".

Pneumonia: Two forms of pneumonia have been observed. An acute form, which can manifest rapidly and without very much in the way of advance warning leading to death within hours if untreated and a chronic form which can manifest just as quickly but which then stabilises and can persist for many weeks months or even years. Of the two types the acute form is by far the easiest to treat as it generally responds to readily available antibiotics and even cases in a state of unconsciousness and near death can make almost miraculous recoveries when so treated. The following drugs and dosing schedules have proved satisfactory when dealing with this type of pneumonia;

      Ampicillin - 50mg/kg, dose every 24 hours for 5 days.
      Oxytetracycline - as above.

Both of the above are comparatively safe compared to many other drugs and we have certainly noted no serious adverse effects despite monitoring many administrations over the years. Ampicillin can however cause local swelling at the injection site. In general we have recorded best results with oxytetracycline followed closely by ampicillin. Tylosin at 50mg/kg seems particularly safe and effective against mild upper respiratory tract infections, where we have experienced consistently good results. In a case of acute pneumonia however we would have more confidence in oxytetracycline and should no improvement be noted after a few hours on that would rapidly recommend a change to ampicillin. Certainly, we normally expect to see a definite improvement within hours rather than days from an acute phase if the drug is going to work at all. If no improvement is noted within a relatively short time, our inclination is to move on to the next drug of choice. The most important thing when confronted with an animal suffering from an acute pneumonia is to obtain an effective blood serum level of antibiotic as quickly as possible. Keeping the animal at optimum temperatures and maintaining a good state of hydration are also important. Increased temperatures increase metabolic rate and therefore drug take-up as well as stimulating natural immune responses.

The other form of pneumonia is observed less frequently, but is also much more resistant to treatment. Here, only the amino-glycoside antibiotics seem effective and then not always. Roughly 75% of cases in our experience do respond to parenteral treatment with framycetin or gentamycin at 10mg/kg every 40 hours for 7 doses but the remaining 25% continue to show no improvement or are subject to recurrence.

X-ray examinations of the lungs of tortoises affected with this latter type of pneumonia tend to show a diffuse infection sometimes affecting one lung in its entirety. In a small number of cases where all else has failed to bring about improvement our veterinary surgeons have drilled the carapace introducing aminoglycoside antibiotics directly to the affected tissues thus obtaining high densities of active agent where it is needed most. This is obviously an advanced and drastic procedure, but is certainly justified in a limited number of cases. Results have been encouraging, with complete recovery from even the most severe and chronic forms. It is only fair to point out that by no means all cases respond and that the only mortalities we have ever suffered as a result of pneumonia have been among the small number of chronic infections we have encountered. It is perhaps worth highlighting the common symptoms of the two forms of pneumonia for the benefit of readers who might not have encountered the condition.

Acute: Gaping of the mouth is often combined with stretching of the neck and obvious respiratory embarrassment. Excess mucous may or may not be visible in the nares or mouth which may be synotic. There may be weakness in the legs and poor retraction. Dehydration may also feature. Some tortoises may exhibit hyperactivity attempting to run around sometimes seemingly blindly; this may be in an effort to boost metabolic rate or ease breathing. All such cases require antibiotic therapy as a matter of the most extreme urgency. Survival time without prompt and effective treatment is measured in hours not days.

Chronic: May be persistent low level discharge of mucous, mouth may be synotic (mauve from de-oxygenation). Coughing and wheezing might be audible. There may be a lack of strength and poor retraction. Oropharyngeal cultures will frequently reveal resistant strains of Gram-negative bacteria present.

Runny Nose Syndrome (Rhinitis): Can present a major problem to large-scale tortoise breeders and keepers. Uncertain etiology, but probably initiated due to a wide variety of factors of which stress, overcrowding, vitamin-A deficiency and maintenance at inappropriate temperatures and humidity are probably the most important. The design of chelonian housing and vivaria appears to have a major impact on the incidence of this condition. Secondary bacterial infection compounds the initial factors and can lead to formation of a chronic, debilitating condition which can prove extremely difficult to eliminate. It is important to note that the bacteria involved are almost always of the Gram-negative type principally *Klebsiella*, *Pseudomonas* (especially *fluorescens*) and *Citrobacter* (especially *freundi*).

Probably the best advice must be to provide any tortoise suffering with this condition with the closest possible to natural and ideal conditions of temperature and humidity.

Other factors which may yet prove to be implicated in 'RNS' include mycoses and viral agents. Much work remains to be done in this field. However the mere possibility that there could be a viral involvement and the certainty that where bacteria are implicated they tend to be of a particularly resistant type should make it obvious that very careful handling and good quarantine techniques are a pre-requisite when treating such cases.

The study of viral agents as causes of diseases in tortoises is as yet an early stage; however, several *Herpes* type organisms have recently been isolated and it is virtually certain that as research progresses some of the more mysterious and difficult to control conditions which affect these animals will eventually be traced to a viral cause.

Standard procedures for dealing with 'RNS' include the use of nasal antibiotic drops (neomycin, oxytetracycline in suspension or tobramycin) sometimes supplemented with antibiotic injections; best results observed to date have been obtained with oxytetracycline, which has consistently produced a higher clear-up rate than either framycetin or gentamycin.

Finally it is worth checking before recourse is made to drug therapies that the cause of any persistent nasal discharge is not merely a foreign body lodged in the nares. This may seem obvious, but it is surprising how often such a simple cause if overlooked. Another common cause of runny noses is vitamin-A deficiency. Inadequate environmental control is certainly one of the most common causes – especially in the case of north African *Testudo graeca* where maintenance under conditions which are too dry is almost guaranteed to initiate the problem.

Septicaemia and peritonitis

Septicaemia in tortoises is not uncommon. The pathogens mainly responsible are again of the Gram-negative group often *Pseudomonas* and *Aeromonas*. Symptoms of a generalised septicaemia include vomiting, lethargy and sometimes a distinct reddish 'flush' or 'tinge' on the plastron or under the carapace shields (vascular congestion and haemorrhage). A particularly revealing symptom is petechiation of the tongue and mucous membranes with many micro-haemorrhages visible in advanced cases. Some septicemia may be accompanied by acute jaundice, and affected reptiles may drink excessively.

When confronted with these symptoms, the most effective course of action usually is to administer an antibiotic by injection as quickly as possible. Good results have been obtained with framycetin and gentamycin as well as with oxytetracycline and ampicillin (although this latter is not normally a first choice for this condition). The doses used were as described previously.

Septicaemia may result from abscesses or as a result of other infected lesions. In female tortoises problems with eggs are often implicated. Eggs may become 'stuck' or rupture and the female can rapidly deteriorate into a state of full scale egg peritonitis. Symptoms include problems with the back legs, reluctance to walk, lethargy and all the other signs outlined above which are associated with septicaemia. An X-ray examination will confirm the presence of eggs, sometimes highly calcified. The aetiology of the condition is complex but a variety of factors including photo-period, temperature and dietary deficiencies are certainly implicated. One major factor appears to be the practice of hibernating female tortoises with retained eggs. Where possible, this should be avoided. One fatality reported concerned a female *Testudo graeca* which at post-mortem was found to have 14 eggs inside her; – 7 were heavily calcified and were obviously produced during the previous year and had been retained, the rest were relatively fresh.

Treatment presents certain difficulties. Where possible any underlying septicaemia should be treated first using systemic antibiotics. It may then be possible to induce laying by the use of calcium borogluconate and oxytocin injections (the calcium should precede the oxytocin by 12 to 24 hours). The normal dose range for oxytocin in this application is from 1.5 i.u/kg to 10mg/kg supplemented with 0.01 ml/gm of a 1% injectable solution calcium. It definitely helps if the uterine mucosa are lubricated or moist.

Miscellaneous Diseases
The following conditions may or may not be related to bacterial infections. Sometimes they are observed individually, sometimes in combination with other diseases.

Renal failure Symptoms include oedema, pale mucous membranes and lethargy. Reluctance or inability to urinate. Weight may increase drastically due to retention of fluids. Often seen following long term anorexia, dehydration or bacterial infection.

Treatment includes 'flushing' the renal system with compound sodium lactate or pure water. Do not administer oral rehydration therapies. Fluid should be delivered at approximately 5% of total bodyweight daily. Complete renal failure is incurable. Some forms of temporary renal failure respond to treatment as outlined above, or to systemic injection of

68

diuretic drugs (frusemide has proved effective in chelonians). Cases of 'renal constipation' due to concreted uric acid deposits are quite often encountered; regular baths and physiotherapy of the back legs can definitely help to release the offending blockage. In cases of persistent renal constipation due to excessive uric acid production drugs can be prescribed by which will reduce help to reduce this but in the long term strict dietary control is likely to be equally if not more effective.

Hepatic disease Symptoms include acute or recurrent jaundice. Likely cause is secondary abscessing in liver following long term bacterial infection. Treatments include oral administration of the amino-acid Methionine (200mg every 48 hours) for 5 doses and in severe cases systemic injection of anabolic steroid. Total liver failure is incurable, but many cases do respond to the above. The animal should be well hydrated using compound sodium lactate or pure water. Glucose may also help. It should be noted that very many clinical cases of liver disease result directly from incorrect dietary management, especially excessive fat intake or a diet too rich in proteins.

Stress The non-specific nature of stress makes it a difficult problem to address; however, there is no doubt that it is often at the root of many disease problems in captive collections. A stressed animal undergoes a number of biochemical changes, some of which, such as the production of steroids, suppress the natural immune system. Thus, stressed animals are many times more likely to succumb to whatever pathogens they are exposed to than healthy, non-stressed animals exposed to the same organisms. Stress can be reduced in several ways;

∗ By maintaining animals under as natural conditions as possible.

∗ By providing a good diet.

∗ By not subjecting sensitive animals to aggressive behaviour by other, more competitive animals.

∗ By reducing overcrowding and, in the case of females, by making certain that nesting site selection is not unduly stressful.

Stress in tortoises is not easy to detect – until it is too late. By taking preventative steps early enough, many disease problems and fatalities can be completely avoided.

(1) Notes on Handling
All cases of bacterial (or worse, viral) infection must be handled extremely

carefully with regard to the risk of cross infection. Use effective antiseptics liberally and do not under any circumstances allow infected (or suspect) animals to come into contact with others. Isolation facilities are absolutely essential. Wash hands between every handling, and prepare food separately. Surgical gloves are useful where handling open wounds and particularly infectious cases.

(2) Notes on Antibiotics

Mention has been made above of various antibiotic agents and dose rates. The following chart summarises these notes and provides a few more details based on several years extensive observations. It is important to note that all antibiotic drugs should only be used under the direction of a qualified veterinary surgeon.

Tylosin (50mg/Kg). Fairly safe. Good results in mild respiratory infections reported.

Oxytetracycline (50mg/Kg). Fairly safe although can cause some irritation at injection site, also a tendency to cause digestive upset. Very good to excellent results in cases of respiratory infection.

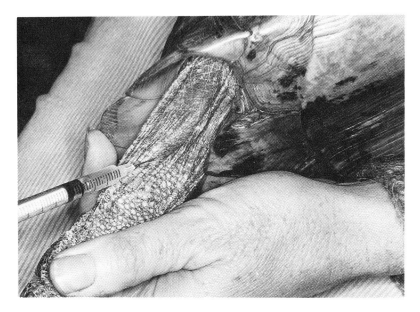

The muscle at the top of the rear legs is usually the preferred site for injections.

70

Amoxycillin (oral suspension, as per veterinary direction). A useful drug in cases of stomatitis where good results are consistently obtained. Rapid absorption into bloodstream. One of the few antibiotics where oral dosing is recommended.

Ampicillin (50mg/Kg). Can cause severe injection site irritation. Fairly safe. Reasonable to good results in cases of pneumonia and septicaemia.

Chloramphenicol (50mg/Kg) Good results against some Gram-negative infections.

Framycetin (10mg/Kg) Very effective against septicaemia not quite so effective against acute respiratory disease but better in chronic pneumonia than oxytetracycline. No side effects observed if safe doses employed.

Gentamycin (10mg/Kg). As above but seems to be better than framycetin in cases of acute pneumonia.

Tobramycin (10mg/Kg) As above.

Amikacin (10mg/Kg) As above.

Netilmycin (10mg/Kg) As above.

Note that aminoglycoside antibiotics should NOT be used in combination with frusemide or with any neuromuscular blocking drug. Where renal function is impaired, they may only be used with the most extreme caution.

All above (except amoxycillin) are listed as per systemic subcutaneous injection. Oral dosing is generally not recommended in tortoises as it can be difficult to calculate eventual blood serum level and the antibiotics can have a serious effect upon gut flora if delivered by this route. Where possible (i.e in strictly local infections) a topical application is generally to be preferred, e.g cloacitis responds well to framycetin paste per cloaca, and ocular infections are generally best treated with eye ointment or drops. The only exception to the general prohibition on oral dosing is in cases of severe intestinal bacterial diseases (which are very rare in tortoises) or when eliminating salmonella where no other effective method is practical.

Chapter Nine

Captive Breeding & Species Profiles

The information which follows is intended as a concise and practical guide to the basic requirements of some of the more commonly encountered species from both temperate and tropical climates. It is not intended as a 'complete' guide to the maintenance and breeding of these species; it should however provide a good starting point and serve as a basis for further experimentation and progress in their captive husbandry. Most of the data presented is based upon actual records obtained from successful breeding groups and field studies of the species in the wild.

Under the heading of each species or genus I have included a short taxonomic note. This is necessarily very brief, although in some instances the status of the taxon may be anything but straightforward. Where this is the case, I have included (I hope) sufficient information to enable identification for captive breeding purposes and enough description to avoid inadvertent hybridisation between questionable forms. Readers who require further data on the present taxonomic status of the various species are referred to the select bibliography which is organised by genus for ease of use and, in respect of the Mediterranean species, to my forthcoming "Tortoises of the Mediterranean" which includes a comprehensive survey of this regions species including field data on their distribution and comparative ecology (R & A Publishing Ltd., in preparation).

Leopard tortoise *Geochelone pardalis babcocki*.

Kinixys – African Hinge-back Tortoises

General observations: Members of the genus *Kinixys* are distinguished by their uniquely hinged carapace which allows the rear of the shell to close giving additional protection to the tail and legs; a character which sets them apart from all other terrestrial tortoises.

Taxonomy: The status of *Kinixys* species is, at the present writing, in a state of considerable flux. Until only recently three species had been recognised by most authorities; *Kinixys belliana, K. homeana* and *K. erosa*. These last two being clearly distinguishable from the former. *Kinixys belliana* was assumed to have a wide distribution, from Senegal and northern Cameroon, via southern Africa to Madagascar; as is often the case where wide distributions are assumed, this in fact appears not to be the case. This apparently extensive distribution is illusory, and what passed for 'identical' *"Kinixys belliana"* in much of its assumed range actually comprises populations formed not only of several different subspecies, but also no less than 3 additional full species! In many respects a situation which finds a parallel in north Africa with regard to *Testudo graeca*. The current checklist for *Kinixys* (based upon the pioneering work of Donald G. Broadley with this genus) therefore includes *Kinixys homeana, K. erosa, K. belliana belliana, K. belliana nogueyi, K. belliana zombensis, K. spekii, K. lobatsiana* and *K. natalensis*. It is quite likely that as studies progress additional forms will be identified. From the captive breeding point of view it is readily admitted that such a profusion of species creates some difficulties – not the least of which is obtaining a satisfactory identification of specimens. Fortunately, those species most likely to be encountered under captive conditions, *K. homeana, K. erosa* and *K. belliana belliana* are relatively easy to identify and in the case of unusual specimens study of specialist works on South African chelonia should provide the answer.

Description: The maximum dimensions recorded for male *K. belliana belliana* are SCL (straight carapace length) 206mm and for female specimens 217mm. The carapace is a dull yellow-buff colour with darker brown or reddish-brown central scute markings. The upper posterior section of the carapace is gently rounded. *Kinixys homeana* and *K. erosa* are very different from *K. belliana* in overall appearance, being an overall reddish-brown colour with lighter rather than darker centres to the scutes, and in both cases these tortoises are much more sharply angular at the rear portion of the carapace than *K. belliana*. This characteristic is much more marked in *K. homeana* than in *K. erosa* and may be used to separate the two: in *K. homeana* there is typically a vertical descent from the 5th vertebral scute to the supracaudal. *Kinixys erosa* is the largest of the hinge-backs, with males often exceeding 315mm and females 250mm.

74

LIST OF PLATES

PLATE 1

1. Mating in almost all tortoises is accompanied by vocalisations from the male as he mounts the female *Geochelone (Asterochelys) radiata.*

2. The eggs are laid in a carefully excavated pit.

3. In this half-formed embryo the blood vessels linking the developing tortoise to the yolk can be clearly seen. The head and ribs of the embryo are also easily identifiable.

4. The first stage of hatching; the tortoise pierces the egg using its egg caruncle.

5. Gradually, the hole is enlarged.

6. The tortoise eventually leaves the egg.

PLATE 2

7. Upon hatching, most tortoises are somewhat folded following confinement in the egg. The plastron straightens out within a few days. A rudimentary yolk-sac is also visible.

8. One of the first actions of many hatchlings is to eat some of their own eggshell in an effort to obtain calcium.

9. The juvenile maintenance area at the Charles Darwin Centre on the Galapagos Islands where endangered giant tortoises are bred in captivity.

10. The S.O.P.T.O.M. tortoise conservation centre in southern France which is working to protect *Testudo hermanni hermanni.*

11. During scientific studies these *Testudo hermanni hermanni* from the same population were captured, marked, measured and then released. Note the striking similarity between each individual.

12. A typical captive situation revealing many of the more commonly encountered mistakes; overcrowding, likely contamination of food, a mainly lettuce and tomato diet and a genetically incompatible mixture of various mediterranean species. If breeding occurs here, it's through luck not design!

PLATE 3

13. Typical habitat of South American and tropical forest tortoises.

14. Typical habitat of north African *Testudo graeca.*

15. Typical habitat and nesting site of *Testudo hermanni.*

16. Necrotic stomatitis or 'mouth rot'. This serious bacterial disease requires urgent and careful treatment.

17. Ear abscess. Note the grossly distended tympanitic membrane of this *Terrapene carolina triunguis* (three-toed box turtle).

18. Ulcerative shell disease, or 'shell rot'.

1

4

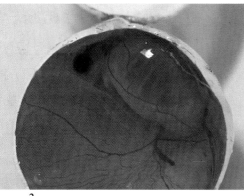

2

5

3

6

Plate 1

7

10

8

11

9

Plate 2

12

13

16

14

17

15

18

Plate 3

Kinixys belliana belliana. Bell's hinge-back tortoise.

Kinixys homeana. Homes' hinge-back tortoise.

75

K. homeana is a smaller species, with males rarely in excess of 208mm and females 220mm.

Captive environment: It is not easy to generalise the requirements of *Kinixys* specimens, as they inhabit a surprisingly wide range of disparate biotypes from coastal plains and savannah to the edges of forests and swamps. Without knowing the origin of specimens it can therefore be extremely difficult to provide the sort of environment to which the animal is accustomed. Some experimentation is usually required, the environment being adjusted in accordance with the tortoises responses. As a starting point, a relatively high humidity should be provided with a daytime temperature in the order of 24–27° C. Water should be available at all times, as *Kinixys* species like to soak and even swim on occasions. Those from forest habitats (e.g *K. erosa* and *K. homeana*) prefer more shade than those from open or savannah habitats, but all tend to be secretive and appreciate a secure retreat area. Most *Kinixys* tortoises tend to be more active during wet and rainy weather, and in souther Africa *K. belliana* is known to aestivate during very dry periods. These tortoises frequently also show a tendency to feed and become active at dawn and dusk. In good weather *Kinixys* species can be maintained outside successfully in both Europe and the U.S.A. An outdoor pen is generally satisfactory provided it is well planted, kept moist, and has plenty of shade. A heated indoor retreat may however be required on all but the very warmest of summer nights. In cool weather these tortoises are best maintained under tropical greenhouse conditions. In South Africa, *K. natalensis* hibernates during the winter months.

Diet: Kinixys species are typically omnivorous with a marked preference for mushrooms, slugs, snails, mixed fruit (especially banana), and earthworms. A good variety of green plant leaf material should also be provided. In a suitable outdoor enclosure the tortoises will find a high percentage of their food for themselves, spending a considerable time engaged in hunting down snails, worms and fresh shoots of weed.

Breeding: Male *Kinixys* can be very aggressive and it may not be possible to maintain more than one per enclosure. *K. erosa* appear to be the most aggressive of all, and two males will sometimes inflict serious injuries upon each other if allowed to. Mating can likewise be a vigorous affair. Female *K. belliana* may lay more than one clutch during the summer, often at intervals of about 5–8 weeks. A clutch typically comprises between 4–8 eggs, occasionally as many as 10 in the case of large individuals. The eggs are very elongate and usually measure approximately 38mm × 48mm and range from 23g to 32g in weight. There are inexplicable size variations in the literature pertaining to the eggs of *Kinixys belliana* and it seems probable that the various populations (and subspecies) in all likelihood produce eggs which are significantly different when considered statistically in a comparative sense. The hatchlings of *K. belliana* typically measure some 38–47mm SCL and weigh circa 17–25g at emergence – again there are significant differences between the different populations. The carapacial hinge is not evident in hatchlings and juveniles. Artificial incubation is most successfully carried out at circa 30.5° C at a medium-high humidity (recommended 75–80%) in either a type I or II incubator. At 30–31° C the incubation period is typically 90–110 days. In the wild the incubation period is variable according to the time of oviposition; it can take anything up to a year. At lower incubation temperatures the eggs may remain viable, but the incidence of dead-in-shell (DIS) increases and incubation time becomes very extended; in their excellent 'South African Tortoise Book' Richard Boycott and Ortwin Bourquin give an example of one egg which took 10 months to hatch when incubated at 25° C and another egg which took 12 months. This latter publication is, incidentally, highly recommended to anyone keeping South African species in captivity.

Geochelone (Chelonoidis) Carbonaria – **The Red-foot Tortoise**

General observations: This is one of the most common south American tortoises, with a wide distribution from Panama to northern Argentina. The descendants of introduced specimens now colonise a number of Caribbean islands although the population of Trinidad may be a natural one. The species is named on account of the bright red scales which adorn its legs in profusion.

Taxonomy: At the higher level, there is much dispute about whether this species should be attributed to *Geochelone* or whether the sub-genus *Chelonoidis* should be elevated to generic rank to include them. Thus is it not unusual to see them listed under both. With a wide and fragmented distribution, *G. carbonaria* demonstrates considerable morphological variation. This is evident not only in the carapace shape but also in colouration. However, there are no currently recognised subspecies and at present the species is considered homogenous. Even so, in view of the variation already noted caution should be exercised in captive breeding and preferably this should be restricted to specimens from similar geographical origins.

Description: A large and impressive tortoise, mature males typically measure some 300mm SCL and most of the females I have measured appear to be of similar size although much larger examples of both sexes have been reported. The principal dimorphic feature is the narrow 'waist' of males, which according to some observers are reminiscent of an overgrown peanut (page 8). The tail of male specimens is also larger than that of females, and in males also the rear lobe of the plastron exhibits a much wider and flatter anal notch. Colour does vary according to locality of origin, with Venezuelan specimens exhibiting a yellowish plastron with a browner carapace and Argentinean specimens a darker, almost black plastron and carapace. In all cases the central areolae of the scutes are marked with yellow. The head is typically brightly marked with yellow scales, but some Venezuelan specimens possess instead a reddish-orange head.

Captive environment: Red-foot tortoises inhabit grassland savannah and drier forest habitats throughout south America. In only a few localities does it impinge upon true tropical rainforest habitats. In captivity, a moderately dry environment and temperature in the region of 21° C (night) to 27° C (day) will suit most specimens. Access to water should however be provided at all times. In most of Europe and north America Red-foot tortoises can be accommodated out of doors during the warm summer months, at least during the daytime, but in the winter and on

Geochelone (Chelonoidis) carbonaria. Redfoot tortoise.

cool nights indoor accommodation is also essential. A well planted outdoor pen with access to a heated hut or greenhouse is probably ideal for this species which is relatively easy to manage in captivity.

Diet: In the wild these tortoises prefer fallen fruits, flowers, green leaves and will occasionally take carrion when it is encountered. In captivity caution should be exercised when offering banana as they easily become addicted to it and meat products should similarly be very strictly rationed. Over reliance upon both items can result in serious dietary problems developing. Most Red-foot tortoises will readily take melon, orange, mango, vegetable greens and grapes.

Breeding: The mating ritual of Red-foot tortoises is startlingly similar in many respects to that of *T. horsfieldi*; the male advances upon the female, circles her repeatedly, extends his neck near her face whereupon he proceeds to move his head rapidly from side to side with a strange jerky motion. This is accompanied by occasional biting, shoving and ramming actions. Eventually he mounts from behind and during copulation emits an extraordinary sequence of 'clucking' or 'cackling' sounds. Two male tortoises will often engage in combat, and most mating activity occurs either during or just after rain. Nesting and egg laying continues all year. The Red-foot tortoises in our own collection regularly lay eggs which measure on average 45mm long by 42mm wide and which weight some 35-50g grammes. Typically a clutch consists of between 3-5 eggs and a female may lay 2-3 clutches each season. At 30° C in a Type II incubator at moderately high humidity incubation takes on average 150-175 days. The hatchlings measure approximately 46mm long, are 42-44mm wide and weigh between 26-32g.

Geochelone (Chelonoidis) denticulata – **The Yellow-foot or Forest Tortoise**

General: These tortoises are distinguished from *G. carbonaria* principally by the bright yellow-orange (rather than red) scales of the legs. They are also light golden-brown in colour, and much larger. It is widely distributed in S. America and is found in Brazil, Ecuador, Columbia, Guyana, Venezuela, Peru, Guyana and Surinam. Like *G. carbonaria* a population also occurs on Trinidad and in much of its range it exists sympatrically with *G. carbonaria*.

Taxonomy: *G. denticulata* was described earlier than *G. carbonaria* (in 1766 as opposed to 1824) and in many old accounts is to be found listed under the heading '*Testudo tabulata*'. As with *G. carbonaria* there is dispute over its generic attribution. It does not demonstrate the regional variation so evident in *G. carbonaria*.

Description: Yellow-foot or Forest tortoises are considerably larger animals than Red-foot tortoises; the average mean adult SCL is 400mm but some very much larger specimens are occasionally encountered. The record is believed to be circa 700mm.

Captive environment: *G. denticulata* inhabit true tropical and sub-tropical forest habitats; as such, they require higher humidity and more stable temperatures than *G. carbonaria*. Continuous access to drinking and bathing water is essential, and a frequent spray with 'artificial rain' is also helpful in maintaining good health and normal activity. Day and night temperatures in the order of 25–27° C are recommended.

Diet: As for *G. carbonaria*.

Breeding: Although superficially similar to *G. carbonaria*, Auffenberg has pointed out that the head movement differs in *G. denticulata*, consisting of a single sweep rather than in a series of jerky motions. Male *G. denticulata* also lack the 'waist' of *G. carbonaria*. Clutch densities have been reported as higher than *G. carbonaria*, as many as 15 on occasions, although most specimens appear to lay between 4–5. In the wild this tortoise does not appear to nest in the normal way, often leaving the eggs at least partially exposed. The eggs are similar in size to those of *G. carbonaria* and can be incubated under identical conditions. If anything, humidity should be a little higher. The hatchlings are very similar in both size and overall appearance to those of *G. denticulata*; so much so that it is not easy to tell them apart. At 30° C the incubation period is usually between 140–160 days.

Gopherus (Xerobates) – American Gopher Tortoises

General: Because of their north American and Mexican location, Gopher tortoises have attracted considerable interest and much scientific investigation; this has resulted in their being among the best known of all land tortoises. However, also because of their proximity to humankind they are under severe pressure from collecting and from habitat destruction. All species of Gopher tortoise are now protected by law and should not be disturbed. Large numbers remain in captivity, both in private and institutional hands and therefore they attract considerable interest from prospective captive breeders. It should be noted that the 'obvious' solution of releasing the large captive population back into the wild to replenish decling stocks is both genetically and biologically highly inadvisable. Under no circumstances should captive specimens be simply turned loose. Not only do they pose a potential genetic risk, but recent evidence suggests that they may contaminate already endangered natural populations with fatal pathogens.

Taxonomy: Until recently it was generally thought that the taxonomy of Gopher tortoises was relatively straightforward; this has in fact proved to be very far from the truth. Four allopatric species are recognised in most recent accounts; *Gopherus agassizi* (the Desert tortoise), *Gopherus berlandieri* (the Texas tortoise), *Gopherus polyphemus* (the Florida gopher tortoise) and *Gopherus flavomarginatus* (the Mexican or Bolson tortoise) which was itself only discovered in 1888 and not fully verified until 1959. Very recently however this apparently simple picture has been completely overturned by studies which suggest that in fact *G. agassizi* and *G. berlandieri* should be considered separately under the generic name *Xerobates*, with only *G. polyphemus* and *G. flavomarginatus* continuing under *Gopherus*. Considering that *Gopherus (Xerobates)* are probably the most intensively studied tortoises in the history of herpetology, that such discoveries are still being made says much for our knowledge of the rest! Even as this book goes to press, reports (as yet unconfirmed) of the discovery of a possible 5th species of tortoise in Baja, Mexico are being received. Not only that, but further (mitochondrial DNA) results indicate that *X. agassizi* itself appears to comprise at least three genetic assemblages in discreet geographical zones as divergent from each other as *X. agassizi* is from *X. berlandieri*; clearly these tortoises have a far from simple ancestry, and a great deal of work still needs to be done if their phylogeny is finally to be unraveled.

Description: Xerobates agassizi; SCL to 380mm, although most much smaller with females smaller than males. This species is principally distinguished by its narrow head and large hind feet. Carapace colouration is light chocolate brown. *Gopherus polyphemus*; this tortoise is

Xerobates berlandieri. Texas gopher tortoise.

externally somewhat similar to *X. agassizi*, of almost identical colour, but the head is much wider and typically the animal is smaller (circa 250mm although some much larger specimens are encountered). *Xerobates berlandieri*; this is the smallest of the Gopher tortoises attaining a typical adult SCL of 160mm SCL although some larger specimens are seen (to about 215mm). The scutes have a much darker brown ground colour than *X. agassizi* (often virtually black), but feature prominent yellowish central areolae; these can however be less obvious in very ancient specimens. The gular projection is very well developed in males, less so in females. *Gopherus flavomarginatus*; this tortoise is the largest terrestrial chelonian in north America, and attains the very considerable SCL of 400mm and weighs in excess of 14kg. It has two very large black black-pointed 'spurs' on the thighs, a brown and yellow carapace with yellowish-horn coloured plastron and the rear marginals are markedly flared and serrate.

Captive environment: All Gopher tortoises are very highly adapted to their native habitat conditions and are by no means easy to maintain successfully - especially outside their natural bioclimatic range. In addition, the various species do differ considerably in terms of temperature and humidity requirements. There are however common threads, one of which is their distinctive habit of residing in burrows – these can be up to 8

83

meters long in the case of *G. flavomarginatus*, and up to 14m long in the case of *G. polyphemus* (although *X. berlandieri* burrows rarely extend for more than 30-40cm). Not only do these provide a means of retreating from unfavourable weather conditions generally, but they provide a microclimate where humidity as well as temperature are relatively stabilised.

In captivity, all Gopher tortoises tend to do badly if overcrowded and if mixed at random with other species. Ideally, they should be provided with an outdoor area of light but excavatable soil, lightly planted with scrub, grass and succulents. An overnight shelter is essential, a small wooden hut is generally satisfactory if provided with a ramp for exit and entry. An even better option is to provide a natural or artificial burrow. Damp environments are categorically not suitable for Gopher tortoises – with the possible exception of *X. berlandieri* which I have found to positively thrive under more humid conditions and *G. polyphemus* which also prefers a relatively high level of ambient humidity. Cold and damp however are definitely to be avoided. In general however, most Gopher tortoises prefer it hot and dry, and will readily take advantage of both natural sunlight and artificial basking facilities. The only moisture in desert tortoise accommodation should comprise the drinking pool – this should be 25-35mm deep and the water changed daily.

Gopher tortoises hibernate during the winter (usually from November or December through March). The best place for such hibernation is a natural or artificial burrow. Temperatures for hibernation are as described previously and are similar to those for *T. graeca* and *T. hermanni*.

Diet: In their native habitat Gopher tortoises are virtually 100% herbivorous, with *X. berlandieri* alone showing some interest in the occasional snail and chance piece of carrion. The bulk of their diet consists of grasses and low growing herbs, flowers, succulents and cacti; *Opuntia* pads and fruits are especially favoured but grasses generally comprise more than half of the total dietary intake. In captivity it is vitally important that the basic chemical balance and profile of the natural diet is followed as closely as possible, even if exactly the same constituents may not be available (see Appendix I).

Breeding: In such a diverse group of animals as the Gopher tortoises it is hardly surprising that considerable variation is found between the various forms in respect of their reproductive biology; *X. agassizi* typically lays clutches of 4-8 eggs (sometimes as many as 14) each approximately 39mm × 44mm. Incubation in the wild takes approximately three and a half months. In captivity, they can be successfully incubated artificially at 30-31° C in a type I incubator at low to medium humidity which typically results in emergence at 80-130 days. The hatchlings typically measure about 48mm SCL and weigh circa 23g. *X. berlandieri* have a lower average clutch density typically depositing 3 or 4 eggs – sometimes as few as 1, just occasionally as many as 5. The eggs from a single clutch may be also laid in different nests, singly. These eggs are quite different from those of *X. agassizi* and when freshly laid are somewhat pliable. They rapidly harden to normal consistency, are markedly elongate and usually measure circa 48mm × 35mm. The hatchlings are smaller than those of *X. agassizi*, measuring on average 40mm long and weigh about 21g. Somewhat surprisingly considering the shape of their egg, they are rounder and less elongate than *X. agassizi* hatchlings. They can be incubated at the same temperature as *X. agassizi* eggs but seem to require a much higher level of ambient humidity throughout the incubation process if embryonic dehydration is to be avoided. A Type II incubator is recommended for this species. *Gopherus polyphemus* lays much more spherical, hard-shelled eggs measuring approximately 40mm in diameter in clutches ranging from 4 to 7. The incubation period in the wild varies from 80–110 days but little data is available on incubation times under artificial conditions. *Gopherus flavomarginatus* are unlikely to be encountered in captivity as it is estimated that the total world population is less than 10,000 individuals. However, their eggs, which closely approximate those of *X. agassizi* in size can be incubated under very similar conditions. It is interesting to note that the conservation captive breeding program for this tortoise in Mexico has made extensive and routine use of oxytocin injections to induce egg laying (see p. 68).

Terrapene – American Box Turtles

General: Box tortoises are so named because they have unusually kinetic plastral hinges which in most cases enable to tortoise to withdraw completely behind a protective "draw-bridge". The locaion of these hinges are important, as they must not be confused with Hinge-back (*Kinixys*) tortoises which achieve a similar result but by means of a hinge in the rear of the carapace. This is an effective defence mechanism and examples of the same evolutionary solution to a common problem are found not only in the New World genera *Terrapene* and *Rhinoclemys*, but also in the Asiatic genera *Cuora* and *Cyclemys* (*Pyxidea*).

Taxonomy: American box turtles belong to the Emydid genus *Terrapene*. In the U.S two species occur each of which is further divided into sub-species as follows; *Terrapene carolina* which is currently considered to have four geographical subspecies – *Terrapene carolina carolina* (the common or Eastern box turtle), *T. c. triunguis* (the Three-toed box turtle), *T. c. major* (the Gulf Coast box turtle) and *T. c. bauri* (the Florida box turtle). The second U.S species is *Terrapene ornata* which has two subspecies – *Terrapene ornata ornata* (the Eastern ornate box turtle) and *T. o. luteola* (the Salt Basin or Texas ornate box turtle).

Description: Box turtles have characteristically high domed carapaces which in some forms is somewhat ridged or keeled in the vertebral region. *Terrapene carolina carolina* occurs from Maine to the deep south; it is quite variable in colouration, but often features yellow or orange streaks and blotches on a brown coloured ground. *T. c. triunguis* occurs in Georgia, eastern Texas and Missouri; again it is variable in colour, some specimens are merely olive or reddish brown whilst others display a fine pattern of radial flecks on a brown-red ground. Its main diagnostic feature is that it has three toes on its hind legs rather than the usual four – although this is by no means an infallible indicator and it is not always easy for the inexperienced observer to tell *T. c. carolina* and *T. c. triunguis* apart. They are both of similar proportions, most adults attaining circa 120–130mm SCL and weighing around 470g. Indeed, any description of U.S. Box turtles can only be regarded in a general sense as a great deal of hybridisation appears to occur between certain races and evident intergrades are frequently encountered. The Gulf Coast box turtle, *T. c. major* is very much more distinctive in both appearance and size. This, the largest of the U.S. box turtles, occurs from south-west Georgia to eastern Texas. A female specimen in our own collection measures 160mm SCL and weighs 635g. *T. c. major* is uniformly dark in colour, almost black, with radiating light marks and blotches on the carapace although these can be absent on some individuals. The feet of *T. c. major* are more

86

Terrapene ornata. The Ornate box turtle.

Terrapene carolina major. Gulf coast box turtle.

evidently webbed than in other members of the *T. carolina* group. The last of the *T. carolina* assemblage is *T. c. bauri*, the Florida box turtle. The carapace of this race is similar in appearance to that of *T. ornata*, but typically the plastron is unpigmented and featureless and it boasts two yellow head stripes in contrast to the characteristic orange-white irregular spotting of *T. c. triunguis* and *T. c. carolina*. The Ornate box turtle, *Terrapene ornata* is a similar, very attractively marked species normally featuring distinctive bright green-yellow eyes. This Box turtle's feet show little evidence of webbing, a testimony to its more typically terrestrial habits than *T. carolina*. The two subspecies are very similar, but are considered separate on the basis of a lack of plastral pattern, typically less distinct carapace radiations and yellowish head scales in *T. o. luteola*. This yellow colouration is more evident in females than males which are typically a more greenish yellow colour.

Captive environment: The various species and subspecies of U.S Box turtle occupy a variety of alternative habitats. These range from open woodlands in the case of *T. carolina carolina* to wet marshes in the case of *T. c. major*; given such a range of habitat preferences it is difficult to generalise even for a single species. However, despite their inclusion in the Emydid family they are all basically terrestrial in habit. From the captive point of view, the main essential variable is the degree of preferred humidity and the time spent in or very near water. Some Box turtles, notably *T. c. bauri* and *T. c. triunguis* are more aquatic than others; these turtles will swim in a pond and even dive to the bottom to forage among the weeds. They are most active in warm, wet weather – thunderstorms are especially welcomed. Others, including *T. ornata* seem to prefer somewhat drier conditions, *T. ornata* in particular is essentially a prairie species with a preference for pastures and open woodlands. All *Terrapene* species can be safely maintained out of doors in the U.S.A and most of Europe at least during the spring, summer and early autumn months. The advice sometimes given that a vivarium environment is ideal is not true. Provided outdoor temperatures are approximately similar to those experienced in their native habitat, then an outdoor environment is infinitely preferable. The Tortoise Trust has maintained all the U.S species of Box turtle in an outdoor terrarium area, very successfully, for several years. A vivarium environment is only employed with sick animals or those we wish to place under observation or to isolate for any reason. A good outdoor terrarium should provide several square meters of land area, a reasonable sized pond for drinking and swimming, and should be thoroughly escape and predator proof – ours is constructed of plywood with a removable wire-mesh top cover. One part can be glazed, thus creating a 'mini-greenhouse' for extra warmth. A good range of weeds and plants should be allowed to grow within the terrarium, and some hollowed out logs make ideal hides and retreats. Box turtles are generally shy creatures, and need to feel secure in order to feel well and to breed. Box turtles do hibernate, typically from November to March. We normally allow the Tortoise Trust colony to hibernate out of doors naturally, the turtles burying themselves deeply under some large half rotted logs in mud, loam and leaf litter. There are reliable accounts of some Box turtles choosing to hibernate over winter buried in the bottom mud of iced over ponds; this is not a procedure which should be encouraged under normal captive conditions as natural ponds are biologically active to a much greater extent than artificial ones and anoxia could very easily occur if conditions are anything less than absolutely ideal. If they are to be overwintered, then a humid vivarium at a minimum of 21° C is necessary with additional basking facilities and preferably equipped with full spectrum fluorescent lighting. Do not allow it to become too dry, or ear and eye problems are almost certain to develop. In the wild, under prolonged drought or heat-wave conditions Box turtles aestivate, disappearing underground for weeks on end.

Diet: Terrapene species are omnivorous. In the wild they consume not only berries and other fallen fruit but also snails, insect larvae, earthworms, crickets, tadpoles, slugs and beetles in addition to toadstools and green plant material. Juveniles are noticeably more carnivorous in nature than fully grown adults. In captivity, if a natural outdoor type environment is adopted then a certain amount of the turtles dietary needs will also be met from natural resources; our own colony can often be observed hunting for small prey in the early morning and late evening, especially during or just after a heavy rainfall. Some supplementary feeding is however essential. This should comprise a wide range of berries and fruits such as cherries, apple, banana or melon plus additional vegetables and salad materials including cauliflower, green and red sweet peppers, lettuce, tomato, mushrooms and even surplus cooked potato. The animal protein requirement can be met from low fat dog food and whole dead mice, locusts and snails. Cat food is not recommended as a staple item as it is dangerously high in fat content. The food should be liberally dusted with a high ratio calcium supplement to counter the high levels of phosphorous present in the animal matter.

Breeding: Sexing box turtles can be somewhat difficult; however, in *T. carolina* males tend to have a red eye whilst females have a yellowish brown eye; sometimes this also applies to *T. ornata* (especially *T. o. luteola*) but by no means always as a bright yellow-green eye is more usually seen in this species. Males also have longer and thicker tails than do females. There is some difference in plastral concavity, typically very evident in the *T. carolina* group but entirely absent in *T. ornata*. American Box turtles can all be captive bred under virtually identical conditions. *T. c. carolina* and *T. c. triunguis* for example typically lay 3-5 elongate eggs (occasionally as many as 8) which are somewhat leathery in texture and on average measure approximately 32mm by 20mm. These should be incubated in a Type II incubator at high humidity in a sphagnum moss substrate. If incubated at 26-28° C hatching usually occurs in 70-85 days. The hatchlings, on average, measure 28mm SCL. If the eggs are allowed to become too dry during the incubation process then embryonic dehydration will occur and the eggs will crumple and collapse. The mating process of *Terrapene* species is most curious; at one stage the males legs frequently become trapped in the posterior plastral hinge of the female – the process can also take several hours in contrast to the very rapid mating procedure of most terrestrial tortoises. This is preceded by a more typical biting, circling and shoving phase – during which the males frequently use their front legs to 'spin' the females around.

Geochelone pardalis – The Leopard Tortoise

General: The Leopard tortoise is the second largest African mainland tortoise (after *G. sulcata*). The largest male ever recorded measured 656mm and weighed 43kg. The largest recorded female measured 498mm and attained a weight of 20kg. Most are substantially smaller, but it is not unusual to find specimens of both sexes in the 350–450mm length range and weighing above 15kg. *G. pardalis* occur from Sudan and Ethiopia and extend their range throughout southern Africa. It is named on account of its strikingly marked carapace which in practice constitutes an excellent camouflage.

Taxonomy: The only currently disputed area of *G. pardalis* taxonomy concerns its division into two sub-species; *G. pardalis pardalis* and *G. pardalis babcocki*. Not all authorities accept that two clearly defined geographical races do in fact occur. However, the evidence for them is fairly compelling. What is not clear, and what might be the cause of at least some of the confusion, is whether these are the only races; certainly some keepers and field-workers I have spoken to are convinced that there may be more. Intergrades are in any case reported which further confuses the situation. There are consistent reports of infertility between pairs which are dissimilar in appearance although which theoretically belong to the same sub-species. The best fertility is obtained from pairs which are visually very similar in terms of overall body morphology, colouration and marking. Of the two recognised forms, *G. p. pardalis* occupies a limited range in Cape Province and in the southwestern sector of the Orange Free State, whereas *G. p. babcocki* (sometimes known as the tropical leopard tortoise) enjoys a much wider distribution and appears to be subject to a higher degree of morphological variation than its Cape relative.

Description: Whilst juveniles of the two currently recognised subspecies are relatively easy to differentiate, the same is not always true of adults. In juveniles, *G. p. pardalis* feature two or more blackish dots in the centre of the costal and vertebral scutes whereas *G. p. babcocki* typically feature only one. In the nominate form the plastral scutes are typically blotched with margins; in *G. p. babcocki* the plastron is typically plainer and lacks the central spots. In adults *G. p. pardalis* are said to be typically flatter than *G. p. babcocki* which is highly domed as well as being considerably smaller in most cases although this last stated character does not coincide with my own observations; I have seen some extremely large *G. p. pardalis*.

Captive environment: In good weather *G. pardalis* should be allowed as much access to an outdoor grazing area as possible. Shade in the form of low growing shrubs and bushes should be included to allow retreat from the mid-day sun. During cold weather and over winter, a large heated shed, greenhouse or indoor penned area is essential which should attain daytime temperatures in excess of 20° C if activity is to be mainained. Spot or infra-red basking facilities will usually be quickly taken advantage of. Overnight temperatures should remain in excess of 10° C. In the wild, the southern race *G. pardalis pardalis* is known to hibernate or at least to experience a winter dormancy period, often seeking retreat from the cold in other animals' discarded burrows. In captivity, most keepers prefer to keep the animals alert and feeding over winter by means of artificial light and heat.

Diet: Leopard tortoises are very typical grazing herbivores; in the wild their diet consists very largely of grasses and succulents such as prickly pear. Several authors refer to their consuming bones and hyena faeces for their calcium content. In captivity *G. pardalis* should be maintained on a diet very high in fiber otherwise diarrhoea and intestinal parasite problems will quickly be encountered. For some years I have maintained a colony of seven *G. pardalis babcocki* on a diet consisting of natural graze (grass and assorted weeds) supplemented with cabbage and other coarse green leaf material in the winter when graze became in short supply. To supply fluid, a few tomatoes and cucumbers are included from time to time. This basic diet is heavily supplemented with 'Vionate' and 'Nutrobal' as these very large (and rapidly growing) tortoises have a prodigious demand for calcium.

Breeding: Leopard tortoises, if provided with good accommodtion and a well balanced diet, can be induced to breed quite readily in captivity. Males and females can be diagnosed by a number of characters; in males the tail is longer and the hind section of the plastron is depressed (only very slightly so in the case of *G. p. babcocki*); males are also somewhat more elongate and narrower than females. In *G. p. babcocki* the males are smaller than females, whilst in *G. p. pardalis* males tend to be larger than females. Males kept together will often fight, levering at each other with the gular until one or other desists in defeat. Males court females in a similar manner, with much pushing and battering with the gular. Finally, the male mounts the female and accompanies the process with a great deal of deep throated 'croaking' and 'grunting'.

Females carrying eggs may go off their food for a while immediately prior to laying, and may dig one or more 'trial nests' in sunny areas of open ground. The nest itself usually measures about 25cm deep and accommodates the typical clutch of 8–10 eggs. Again, differences in clutch size are reported between the two recognised forms with *G. p. pardalis* typically laying more eggs than *G. p. babcocki*. However, the absolute maximum recorded clutch size for *G. p. pardalis* is 18 eggs whilst figures as high as 30 have been reported for *G. p. babcocki* which appears to contradict this. The rounded eggs of *G. p. pardalis* typically measure some 43mm in diameter and weigh 50g or more whilst those of *G. p. babcocki* often are said to be smaller at circa 35mm with a typical weight of only 25g. However, this does not accord with my own observations based upon Kenyan and Tanzanian specimens where the average egg size is closer to 42mm with a weight of 45g. The hatchlings are also claimed to differ in size, those of *G. p. babcocki* at about 38mm in length and weighing circa 17g whilst those of the southern race are said to be somewhat larger at approximately 48mm in length and up to 35g in weight. Once again however I know of 46mm hatchlings which weighed 33g produced by a female of Kenyan origin. Females may go on to produce several clutches per season – as many as six totalling 52 eggs in all has been recorded. Incubation times in the wild are very variable, from 178 days in Zambia to 384 days in Natal. Eggs incubated artificially in a type I incubator at 28° C hatch in about 180 days; at 30° C hatchlings can be expected from 130 days onwards but most often emerge between 140–155 days after laying. Incubation humidity should be moderate. From the moment when the egg is first pierced by the hatchling it may be many hours or even days before it is finally ready to leave the egg; this is true of most tortoises including all *Testudo*, *Furculachelys* and *Geochelone* species. Once the immediate demand for oxygen has been met, the hatchling may remain in the egg whilst the remains of the egg-sac are absorbed. The only real danger (under normal captive circumstances) during this time is if the tortoise becomes dehydrated or if the mucous-like residue inside the egg literally glues the hatchlings mouth, nose or eyes up; mortality can occur if airways become blocked in this way. The problem is best prevented by maintaining adequate air humidity and by gently swabbing any obstructing matter away from the head and front legs using a damp cotton bud. Normally, human intervention will not be required but it is as well to be alert to the possibility. Juveniles grow quickly, and can reach sexual maturity within 5–6 years in the case of males, somewhat older in the case of females which typically begin regular egg production as they attain a weight of 8kg or more.

Geochelone elegans – The Indian Star Tortoise

General: One of the worlds most distinctive tortoises, this strikingly marked animal has for many years been sought after by collectors and illegal export continues to represent a significant threat along with habitat loss and utilisation for food. It has been recorded infrequently in Pakistan, with the main area of distribution in India and Sri Lanka where population density is said to be still good.

Taxonomy: This tortoise appears to be closely related to the almost unknown *Geochelone platynota* of Burma, from which it differs principally by featuring radiating lines on the plastron and by having more rays on the costals. According to some authorities *G. elegans* has a more conical form to the vertebrals and costals than *G. platynota*, but in fact this character is very variable even within *G. elegans* and may be related to geographical origin.

Description: The maximum recorded size of *G. elegans* is circa 350mm, but most specimens are considerably smaller, usually in the region of 250mm SCL. The carapace features the radiating 'star' pattern from whence it takes its name, a characteristic duplicated on the plastron. Each of the

Geochelone elegans. The Indian Star tortoise.

94

costal and vertebral scutes has a large, yellow central dot surrounded by a series of radiating yellow stripes.

Captive environment: G. *elegans* is found in the wild inhabiting dry, scrub forest areas, the borders of sandy deserts and even man-made wastelands. It also inhabits grassy hillsides and the borders of cultivated areas. It appears in this respect a robust and adaptable species, yet in captivity it is generally regarded as extremely sensitive and delicate. Certainly, it does not mix well with other species and is best maintained in isolated groups. In other respects, the tortoise appears to do well if kept under very similar conditions to G. *pardalis*. In most of western Europe and n. America it can be allowed out of doors in good weather, and an enclosure which is well planted with grass is ideal. Overnight, a heated indoor retreat will generally be required. Otherwise treat as for G. *pardalis*.

Diet: As for G. *pardalis*.

Breeding: G. *elegans* are not a particularly easy tortoise to induce to breed (or even mate) in captivity although it can be done. The most consistently successful captive breeding results have been achieved within the species natural bioclimatic range in India and Sri Lanka. Although this species habitat is typically dry, stony and thorny for most of the year, it is subject to seasonal rains or monsoons; it appears to be the on-set of this rainy season which initiates interest in mating. During this period (which occurs in India in June) the animals become especially active and feed extensively upon the new shoots of vegetation. They can often be seen marching in small groups in some areas, a lone female pursued by several males. In captivity interest in mating can sometimes be stimulated by either a natural downpour or by extensive spraying with a hose.

Males rarely exhibit mutual animosity, and aggression is not often observed in this species. Females are typically larger in size than males (circa 290mm compared to 230mm) and achieve sexual maturity at about 10-12 years of age. Males can demonstrate sexual maturity in 3–5 years under captive conditions. The eggs appear to be of very variable dimensions, although as in most accounts no geographical origin is disclosed for the specimens it could be that size varies with location. Most eggs measure about 42mm × 31mm, although records indicate a range from 38mm to 50mm in length and from 27mm to 39mm in width. Egg weight is similarly variable from 22g to as much as 38g. Females lay several clutches per year, typically three, but sometimes more. A normal clutch consists of 3 to 6 eggs.

Incubation periods in the wild demonstrate considerable variability depending upon how late or early in the season laying occurs; data from captive specimens within the bioclimatic range indicates that it can take as little as 47 days or as long as 147 days. Artificially incubated eggs in a Type I container at 28° C hatch in about 100 days; at 30° C incubation takes circa 75 days. Incubation humidity should be medium to low. The average length of hatchling *G. elegans* is 35mm and the average weight 15-16g (recorded minimum = 12g, recorded maximum = 22g). The hatchlings lack the distinct ray markings of the adults initially, this first becomes really evident at about 12 months of age.

Testudo hermanni – Hermann's Tortoise

General: Testudo hermanni enjoys a relatively wide distribution in the form of two currently recognised subspecies which includes eastern Spain, southern France, Italy and the Balearic islands, the Balkan peninsula, Yugoslavia, Albania, Bulgaria, Romania, Greece and Turkey. It is also found on Corfu, Sicily and Sardinia.

Taxonomy: There are, as indicated above, two currently recognised sub-species of *Testudo hermanni*. However, these are not as frequently cited in most field guides and other works of reference '*Testudo hermanni hermanni*' in respect of the eastern (Balkan) race and '*T. h. robertmertensi*' in respect of the western (French) race. In fact, by virtue of taxonomic priority the western race is actually the nominate form and should be cited as *Testudo hermanni hermanni* GMELIN 1789 with a designated Type Locality of Collobrieres, France. At the same time, the eastern race should be cited as *Testudo hermanni boettgeri* MOJSISOVICS 1889 with a designated Type Locality or terra typica of Orsova, Romania. The western population, *Testudo hermanni hermanni* is relatively homogenous and is certainly very distinctive. The recent discovery of a southern Italian 'miniature' form

Testudo hermanni hermanni. Hermann's tortoise (photographed in southern France).

97

Plastron *T. h. hermanni* (female).

Plastron *T. h. boettgeri* (male).

The characteristic 'tail spur' of *T. hermanni.*

which is extraordinarily small (adults are typically less than 115mm SCL) but which in other respects is visually identical to normal Italian or French *T. h. hermanni* may complicate this state of affairs in time. Even so it is clear that generally speaking the western populations of *T. h. hermanni* are very convergent in all external characters. The same cannot be said of the eastern sub-species *T. h. boettgeri* which is by no means contiguous and which displays an alarming range of shapes, sizes, colours and patterns within what is supposed to be a single (subspecific) form. It is almost certain that further research will eventually lead to the identification of certain populations which will require separate taxonomic consideration. It may also be necessary to view the entire *T. hermanni* conglomerate as a complex of many very divergent individual populations than as two simple and clearly defined geographical sub-species.

Description: *Testudo hermanni* was first differentiated from *T. graeca* on account of the horny tip it bears upon its tail and its lack of thigh tubercles. Unlike *T. graeca*, *T. ibera* and all other mediterranean or asiatic terrestrial species with the exception of *T. horsfieldi* it has a fixed and rigid xiphiplastron. It is typically a flattish animal with a broad, low carapace which bears black markings upon an olive-yellow base. The western population of *T. h. hermanni* are typically smallish tortoises circa 120–130mm SCL whilst certain eastern populations of *T. h. boettgeri* can easily reach double this length. In both cases there is marked dimorphism, with western males attaining a typical absolute maximum of 165mm and females 190mm. I have measured several (female) tortoises from Bulgaria however which exceed 260mm SCL and which weigh in excess of 3,400g. Most of the tortoises of Yugoslavia, although considerably larger than *T. h. hermanni* at an average of 180–200mm SCL do not attain such dramatic dimensions as that. Curiously, these 'giant' Hermann's tortoises from eastern europe have all possessed 4 claws on all feet – a character usually associated with *T. horsfieldi*. Hybridisation is here ruled out, as they do not occur sympatrically in the region. It is frequently alleged that it is possible to distinguish between the western and eastern populations of *T. hermanni* by determining if the supracaudal shield is divided or undivided. It is also sometimes claimed that *T. hermanni* can be distinguished from *T. graeca* using the same criteria. In fact, neither claim is true and this character is of little value in specific determination. The plastral markings of *Testudo hermanni hermanni* are characteristically formed of two almost solid dark bands running longitudinally down the plastron. Every specimen of this sub-species examined by the author (several hundred in both France and Italy) have possessed this feature. The plastral markings of the eastern form *T. hermanni boettgeri* appear to be somewhat more variable. Some specimens examined have possessed plastrons with dense markings which almost approach that of *T. h. hermanni* so this character should not employed in isolation to diagnose speciation. Most bear a diffuse series of blotches however.

The groundcolour of *T. h. hermanni* is typically a bright golden yellow. This contrasts sharply with most specimens of the eastern *T. h. boettgeri* where the groundcolour could best be described as a greenish-yellow. Similarly, the carapace markings of the western population seem to be unusually clear and well defined compared to most eastern specimens.

Captive environment: The natural habitat of *T. hermanni* is evergreen Mediterranean oak forest; this habitat has however been substantially degraded and reduced as a result of human activity. Present-day populations are therefore found in (secondary) maquis type environments coarse, arid and scubby hillsides. In only a very few places does *T. hermanni* continue to inhabit surviving primary forest. In captivity *T. hermanni* is a comparatively resilient and adaptable tortoise. It seems equally at home in arid or even moderately damp environments but plenty of sun and warmth is essential. An ideal captive situation would provide a large outdoor enclosure, planted with low growing herbs and shrubs on well drained soil. There should be a slope or gentle hill to encourage basking and to provide a nesting site. For overnight accommodation, a wooden hut can be provided although most tortoises will make a 'scrape' under a suitable bush. In the wild, *T. hermanni* hibernate from November to April.

Diet: The natural diet of *T. hermanni* consists of herbaceous and succulent plants native to the mediterranean zone. In captivity as wide a range of weeds and green vegetation as possible should be provided. Lettuce alone is far from an adequate substitute. A natural grazing area is much better than artificial feeding. Although most *T. hermanni* enjoy fruits, an excess should not be given as their sugar content can increase the probability of digestive problems and diarrhoea. *T. hermanni* require a diet which is very high in fibre and will often take dried leaves in preference to fresh. Just occasionally in wet weather *T. hermanni* will take advantage of a passing slug or snail but this does not comprise a significant dietary component. They should not be provided with any meat-based food items in captivity; if they are, then serious consequences may be encountered in the long-term. During heavy rain *T. hermanni* raise themselves on their back legs and place their noses to the ground in order to drink from shallow puddles; typically they also void urine at the same time. As with many arid-adapted reptiles they normally choose not to lose fluid unnecessarily until it can be easily replenished. It is important to note that as with all mediterranean tortoises, seasonal variations in the quantity, quality and constituency of the food intake is an important factor; in spring abundant moist food is available in the form of fresh shoots and flowers but in

100

summer the land becomes dry and unable to support much green vegetation. During this period the tortoises consume food with a higher dry-weight ratio than they do earlier in the year. In extreme conditions (as experienced in north African mediterranean zones for example) the tortoises may actually aestivate during this barren period. The early autumn rains result in a renewal of green vegetation allowing for a final feeding period before hibernation.

Breeding: The breeding behaviour of *T. hermanni* is very different from that of all other mediterranean species. Unlike *T. graeca* or *T. ibera* male *hermanni* do not engage in the same degree of violent 'ramming' activity during courtship, instead resorting much more to head and leg biting which can become quite vicious in nature to the extent of occasionally drawing blood. The horny tip of the tail is also used to stimulate the females cloacal region. Males are also frequently observed apparently 'resting' on females backs almost mechanically stroking the carapace of the female with the front legs; this behaviour, which is conducted in a seemingly trance-like state can persist for hours. It is not known what purpose it serves, if any. Mating is a vigorous affair, accompanied by high pitched 'squeaks' from the male during copulation. Egg laying in the wild takes place from April to June and hatching usually occurs immediately following the first rains of September. There is a very marked difference both in clutch density and egg size between the western *T. h. hermanni* and eastern *T. h. boettgeri*; the average clutch size of *T. h. hermanni* in France is 3, whilst in eastern *T. h. boettgeri* it is typically 5–8 and can be as high as 12. The eggs of *T. h. hermanni* are fairly small at 30mm long by 24mm wide on average, whilst those of *T. h. boettgeri* are by comparison enormous at 40mm long by 29mm wide. Hatchling *T. h. hermanni* typically weigh 9–10g or so, whilst eastern *T. h. boettgeri* hatchlings weigh in at an average of 12–14g. Statistically and in taxonomic terms, these are very significant differences. Both sub-species frequently lay more than one clutch per year. In captivity artificial incubation at 30.5–31° C normally results in hatching at about the 8th or 9th week.

Testudo (Agrionemys) horsfieldi – **The Afghan or Steppe Tortoise**

General: The Afghan tortoise has to date been little studied and much remains unclear concerning its biology, taxonomy and ecology. In Pakistan *T. horsfieldi* occurs in Baluchistan and in very low densities in the North West Frontier Province. It also occurs in the U.S.S.R where it is subject to heavy exploitation.

Taxonomy: At the species level there is little dispute; at genus level its taxonomic status is very confused. The morphological evidence is conflicting. The cranial characters suggest a close affinity to *Testudo*, but the carapace osteology is sufficiently different for it to be allocated to the genus *Agrionemys* by several authorities. Externally, it expresses a marked phenetic relationship to *T. hermanni* with which it shares the morphological features of fixed xiphiplastron and horny tip to the tail – although this latter is reduced compared to *T. hermanni*.

Description: The carapace is typically flattish, roundish and yellow-green or olive in coluration. There are some ill defined dark brown markings on the larger scutes. The plastron is typically blotched with black, or may be black all over on some examples. There is typically a group of enlarged

Testudo (Agrionemys) horsfieldi.

102

scales or tubercles to each side of the tail; these appear to be larger on males than females. The tail has a hard, horny tip. The feet all have four claws. The skin is yellowish. A breeding pair of male and female *T. horsfieldi* now maintained by the Tortoise Trust measure 140mm/590g and 187mm/1,390g respectively.

Captive environment: T. horsfieldi inhabit very arid, barren and rocky areas frequently in excess of 1500m altitude. They burrow deeply into sandy or clay soil in valleys and the walls of dried-up river beds or ravines. They often initiate their burrows under clumps of grass and extend the burrow for up to 2 meters excavating an enlarged chamber at the end. They are most active immediately after hibernation in March and April. In the extreme heat of summer the tortoises spend most of the day in retreat deep within their burrows, often emerging only for an hour or two in the morning or late afternoon to forage. In this, they closely parallel American Gopher tortoises whose lifestyle they in many respects emulate. In captivity, *T. horsfieldi* cannot tolerate damp but otherwise can be successfully maintained under similar conditions to *T. hermanni*. Burrowing facilities should however be provided. This species hibernate during the winter.

Diet: As for *T. hermanni*. Some reports state that *T. horsfieldi* rarely take grass, but I have found that they very much enjoy young green shoots and consume it avidly.

Breeding: In the wild most mating occurs early on in the season. Males are frequently very aggressive. They chase females, biting at their head and legs with sufficient ferocity to regularly draw blood. Two males will often fight viciously if confined together in the breeding season, but at other times seem to co-exist peacefully. Males court females by means of a strange 'head nodding' ritual, staring directly into the females face whilst simultaneously jerking their head up and down in a rapid motion. They emit a series of high pitched squeaks during copulation. The eggs are usually laid within 8 weeks of successful mating, and typically measure some 47mm long by 34mm wide but considerable variability is seen between individual females. Eggs usually weigh between 23-25g. Clutch density is usually between 3-5, but again this is very variable. Two to three clutches are often deposited during a season. In the wild, incubation usually takes 80-110 days, but if incubated at moderate humidity in a Type I incubator at a more or less constant temperature of 30.5°C 60-75 days is more usual. The new hatchlings typically measure between 32-34mm long and weigh from 9-12g. In their first year they tend to grow more quickly than hatchlings of either *T. hermanni* or *T. ibera*.

Testudo ibera – The Spur-thighed Tortoise

General: This tortoise occurs throughout Turkey, north-eastern Greece, Bulgaria, Romania, western Iran, Syria, Jordan, Iraq and the Republic of Georgia in the U.S.S.R. from where the type specimen was taken in 1814. There is a considerable degree of morphological variation throughout this very considerable range, principally in respect of colour but also in size; specimens from asiatic Turkey and Syria tend to be very much lighter and often feature a bright yellow head and limbs. In north-western Turkey *T. ibera* tends to be much more melanistic, and on occasions almost entirely black. An introduced colony of *T. ibera* also exists on Sardinia where it is sympatric with not only similarly introduced *T. hermanni* but also *T. marginata.*

Taxonomy: In 1946 the German herpetologist Robert Mertens designated *Testudo ibera* PALLAS 1814 as a sub-species of *Testudo graeca* LINNAEUS 1758 but this suggestion appears seriously flawed in the light of recent investigations. There are in fact major structural, biotypic and behavioural differences between *T. graeca* and *T. ibera* which Mertens (and most subsequent authors) have completely overlooked. Thus, this tortoise should be considered separately from *T. graeca* which it only very superficially resembles. Within the very large and widely distributed population of *T. ibera* however there are a considerable number of very distinct geographical forms or races some of which occur in relative isolation, some of which appear to represent extremes of clines; only a few of these have so far received separate systematic recognition. To date only *Testudo (graeca) nikolskii* from northwest Transcaucasia and *T. (graeca) anamurensis* from southwestern Turkey have been proposed. It should be noted that although assigned by their respective authors to '*Testudo graeca*' if *T. ibera* is considered a true and separate biological species these would instead be amended to *T. ibera nikolskii* and *T. ibera anamurensis*. Of the lighter coloured and frequently much smaller Syrian and Jordanian forms very little field data currently exists and these are sometimes in error referred to as examples of '*Testudo graeca terrestris*' with which it also allegedly intergrades (for more details of which see under '*T. graeca*').

Description: *T. ibera* is readily distinguished from true *T. graeca*; it is considerably larger with males typically reaching 180mm SCL and females 201mm SCL, although even larger examples are very frequently seen. It is also much broader and flatter than *T. graeca* which is characteristically high domed in lateral profile (the length-height-width ratios of *T. graeca* and *T. ibera* are totally dissimilar). The groundcolour of *T. ibera* is quite variable but ranges from a greenish horn colour to light orange-brown. The carapace markings are brownish-black and the

Testudo ibera. Example from Turkey.

T. ibera hatchling (left), *T. h. boettgeri* (right).

vertebral and costal scutes typically feature a dark central areola with anterior and lateral borders. Very aged specimens sometimes lose the outer layer of keratin revealing large irregular bright orange areas underneath. Another carapace character which also distinguishes *T. ibera* from *T. graeca* is found at the 1st vertebral scute which is very angular compared to the rounded form of *T. graeca*. The head (and underlying cranium) of *T. ibera* is quite different from that of *T. graeca*, the nose in particular is broader and blunter and the eyes are characteristically much larger by comparison. The limbs are by comparison to *T. graeca* much thicker and shorter (there are acute osteological differences involving certain limb bones). The supracaudal shield is only occasionally divided and the thighs feature either a single or double 'spur'. Some geographic populations have significantly flared or serrate posterior marginals, occasionally upturned or reverted, a character which is more prevalent in males than females.

Captive environment: Generally as for *T. hermanni*. *Testudo ibera* are a relatively tenacious and robust species capable of withstanding considerable extremes of climate. Along with *T. hermanni* they tend to do well under captive conditions and breed very readily.

Diet: As for *T. hermanni*.

Breeding: For best breeding success, pairs should be closely matched on the basis of general colouration and markings. Although dissimilar pairs can and do produce viable offspring, this is noticeably less consistent than is the case if pairs are more closely matched. Clutch density ranges from 4-12 but more typically numbers 6-8. Large females tend to produce higher clutch densities than smaller specimens. The eggs of *T. ibera* throughout its range appear remarkably consistent in both size and weight; on average they measure 36mm long by 30mm wide and weigh about 18-20g. They can be incubated in a Type I incubator in a medium humidity environment and at a more or less constant temperature of 31° C can be expected to hatch in 60-80 days. The hatchlings typically weigh in the region of 14-16g and measure 32-34mm SCL. Contrary to popular belief the hatchlings can usually be hibernated without difficulty – indeed, it is preferable that they should hibernate if at all possible. However, under artificial conditions the very greatest care must be taken to ensure temperatures remain at between 4-6° C and that excessive weight loss does not occur. Due to the reduced body mass of hatchlings, their core temperature fluctuates much more rapidly than that of adults in response to sudden environmental temperature changes – a temperature deviation which might cause no problem for a large adult can easily kill a tiny hatchling. Nor should hibernation periods be excessively long –

between 65-80% of the normal typical hibernation period in the wild is usually the advisable maximum. We believe however that even a short hibernation is beneficial – provided it is correctly managed. There is simply no room for error. If overwintering is preferred for the first year, then a heated and illuminated vivarium will be required.

Testudo graeca – The North African or Moorish Land Tortoise

General: Testudo graeca was for years in Europe considered the archetypal 'pet tortoise'. So much so that it became generally known as the 'common tortoise'. However, in reality this creature is little known and is very far from common. It is found only in certain limited areas of north Africa and a small population also occurs in southern Spain. I have examined osteological material of north African descent from the Balearic islands.

Taxonomy: 'Confusing' would be the most appropriate description. Despite being described for the first time in 1758 even today few are aware of its true nature. For many years, *Testudo graeca* was considered to be the only land tortoise in n. Africa with the exception of *Testudo kleinmanni* which is found in Egypt and Libya. Other Mediterranean tortoises were considered to be closely related to it and were thus regarded as sub-species. These included *Testudo (graeca) ibera*, *Testudo (graeca) zarudnyi* and *Testudo (graeca) terrestris*. This latter is itself the subject of yet more taxonomic confusion not to say mayhem in that it sometimes also passes for *Testudo (graeca) floweri* – yet another alleged form which to all intents and purposes is completely unknown and which entirely lacks any adequate type description. Both *T. ibera* and the rarely encountered Iranian *T. zarudnyi* are in this authors opinion full and separate biological species bearing only the most distant relationship to the African *T. graeca*. Meanwhile *T. (graeca) terrestris* simply does not exist in the commonly understood sense. The name is simply a convenient 'catch-all' for a variety of currently poorly defined and little known tortoises which inhabit a herpetologically almost unstudied region. It should be noted that the allegedly 'tiny' terrestris form has never been scientifically described in any meaningful way and that some authors versions of this mysterious creature measure in excess of 250mm SCL! If this situation was not complex enough, it now transpires that the *Testudo graeca* described by Linnaeus is far from the only tortoise species which occurs in north Africa. These recently discovered (or in one case, re-discovered) tortoises are really very different in almost every respect from the Linnaean holotype. It is beyond the scope of this particular book to even begin to describe their complex morphology, osteology and phylogeny; however it is worth noting that at their most extreme these 'new' tortoises include distinct geographical forms which range from 'giants' which attain an SCL of 345mm and weigh almost 5kg (thus equaling *T. marginata* in length and totally eclipsing it in body mass) to true 'pygmy' or miniature species which even as fully grown adults measure only 130mm and weigh less than 400g. Certain aspects of their osteology have caused some to be placed in an entirely new genus *Furculachelys*. Others remain in *Testudo*. The current checklist of north African tortoises

Testudo graeca graeca from Oran, Algeria.

therefore includes not only *Testudo graeca* (Western Algeria and Morocco) and *Testudo kleinmanni* (Libya and Egypt) but also *Furculachelys whitei* (central coastal Algeria), *F. nabeulensis* (Tunisia) and *T. flavominimaralis* (Libya). This latter little tortoise incidentally, with its bright yellow elongate carapace, bright black eyes, bright yellow 'masked' head and yellow scaled legs is one of the several entirely different tortoises which have frequently been mistaken for *Testudo graeca terrestris* on the erroneous basis that as they are obviously not a 'normal' *T. graeca* they can't be anything else!

Description: True *Testudo graeca* are a relatively small tortoise but by no means as small as *T. flavominimaralis* or *F. nabeulensis* from which they differ not only osteologically but also in terms of their external morphology and marking. Males typically attain no more than 145mm SCL (the average is 130mm) and weigh circa 535g. Females are considerably larger and demonstrate a high degree of dimorphism; 180mm SCL and a weight in the region of 1,300g would not be untypical. The carapace is not at all flattish but is highly domed. The groundcolour of the scutes is bright yellow and features an irregular series of small black brown flecks or spots. The areola of each large scute has a central black

109

dot which is bordered laterally and anteriorly. The scales of the head and legs are yellow. The frontal vertebral scute is roundish in form, somewhat pinched in or depressed on the lower half. The rear marginals are not at all flared or serrate, even on males. The superacaudal is not projected and is not ventrally introflexed. There are small tubercles or 'spurs' on the upper thighs, next to the tail.

Captive environment: T. graeca (and all north African species generally) are extremely environmentally sensitive and cannot tolerate any mishandling. They usually tend to do badly in captivity and very few survive in the long-term. If mixed with other more robust, competitive and aggressive species such as *T. hermanni* or *T. ibera* they rapidly succumb to alien diseases and stress. They should be maintained separately. They require conditions of higher ambient humidity than *T. hermanni* or *T. ibera*. In the wild when conditions become too hot and dry they aestivate underground. If deprived of this facility they soon develop respiratory diseases. Some authors have mistaken *T. graeca* aestivating in August (when temperatures regularly soar into the high 90's F) as the beginning of their hibernation period! In fact, some coastal populations do not naturally hibernate at all – it never gets cold enough. The coldest months are January and February where it only just falls below 60° F. In north Africa I have found tortoises grazing and otherwise behaving perfectly normally on Christmas day. Inland populations at the higher altitudes are more inclined to hibernate – but only for a very short while. Extended hibernation periods can be fatal and they should not be subjected to them.

Diet: Similar to *T. ibera, T. marginata* and *T. hermanni* but flowers appear to be a more important dietary constituent. These tortoises are all coprophagous to a greater or lesser extent, feasting whenever the opportunity arises on mammalian dung – in north Africa sheep, goat and camel droppings are all taken with relish. It is quite likely that this does in fact play an important biochemical and digestive role but to date this aspect has been little studied.

Breeding: Unlike *T. hermanni, T. marginata* or *T. ibera*, north African *T. graeca* are rarely bred at all in captivity. In addition, very little data is available on their natural reproductive biology or behaviour. In the last 12 months however the Tortoise Trust has succeeded in captive breeding north African tortoises from several different localities including true *T. graeca*. The eggs are much smaller and rounder than those of *T. ibera* typically measuring 30mm long by 27mm wide. The hatchlings weigh a diminutive 7–8g and measure circa 28mm SCL. A typical clutch consists of 4–5 such eggs. Incubation is best accomplished at between 30.5° C and 31.5° C in a Type I unit at medium humidity. At this temperature range incubation takes approximately 68–80 days. The hatchlings are light brownish-yellow in colour without distinct markings which develop as they grow. By 1 year of age they are approximately half the size of *T. ibera* hatched at the same time.

Furculachelys whitei from Algiers, Algeria.

Furculachelys nabeulensis from Tunisia.

Testudo marginata – The Marginated Tortoise

General: Testudo marginata is one of the largest circum-mediterranean tortoises (comparable only to Algerian *F. whitei* which surpasses it in body mass) and is distinguishable not only by its extremely flared, serrate and projecting rear marginals (from which it takes its name) but also by its unusually marked plastron which is unique among the tortoises of the region (see however my note concerning *T. kleinmanni*). The main population concentration of *T. marginata* occurs in the Peloponnese and along the associated Greek coast to Mount Olympus. Smaller populations occur on several Aegean islands, and an introduced population occurs on Sardinia. A small population also survives to this day in Tuscany, Italy where it is assumed to have been introduced by the Etruscans.

Taxonomy: This tortoise was described by Schoepff in 1792 and has since acquired a number of synonyms including '*T. nemoralis*' and the rather descriptive '*T. campanulata*'. The Marginated tortoise is distinctive both visually and zoogeographically and its status has rarely been the subject of any dispute. Early records of alleged '*T. marginata*' from north Africa (of which, surprisingly, there are plenty) are the result of confusion either with the similarly sized *F. whitei* of Algeria or equally surprisingly with the diminutive *Testudo kleinmanni*; despite all the other differences this little tortoise does feature an approximately similar set of markings on its plastron – not similar enough to cause any confusion you would have thought, but nonetheless this mistake has occurred several times.

Description: In addition to the obviously flared posterior marginals noted above, *T. marginata* feature several other key distinguishing features. The soft skin of the upper limbs and tail is typically very creamy pale; much more so than on either *T. ibera* or *T. hermanni* and very noticeably so in young animals. The plastron of *T. marginata* characteristically features a large brown-black triangular marking on each of the larger scutes. The head is relatively small and the eyes are also smaller and more almond-shaped than those of *T. ibera*. It has been claimed that *T. marginata* has 5 claws on all feet and that the rear plastral lobe is not mobile; neither statement is in fact true. Adult females typically measure circa 240–280mm SCL and weigh on average between 2–3kg, whilst males are normally somewhat longer than females of equivalent age measuring 250–295mm SCL but weigh in the same range. Length for length females typically weigh more than a male of identical SCL but are considerably broader in girth. The assumed homogenous genetic continuity of *T. marginata* is thrown into some doubt however by recent morphometric results which indicate that in at least some populations adult males do not exceed 230mm SCL and females do not exceed 215mm. Other dimorphic

112

Testudo marginata from Greece.

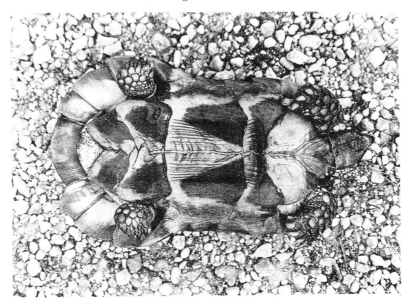

Characteristic plastron pattern of *T. marginata*.

indicators typical of males in this species include tail length, a considerably narrower mid-line and more prominent marginal flares.

Captive environment: As for *T. ibera* and *T. hermanni.*

Diet: As for *T. ibera* and *T. hermanni.*

Breeding: T. marginata breed readily in captivity; possibly the fact that there appears to be relatively little genetic diversity from one part of their range to another (with the exception of the 'miniature' populations noted above) plays a part in this. Certainly, almost any male will mate successfully with almost any female and viable eggs will usually result. Clutch density is typically 8-10 (occasionally more) and the eggs measure on average 30.5mm long by 28mm in width. They normally weigh between 16-18g. If incubated at circa 31° C hatching usually occurs in 60-70 days. Incubation humidity does not appear to be especially critical, good results having been noted in low (- 65%), medium (80%) and high (90% +) environments. One of the most successful breeders of *T. marginata* I know has used a simple Type II incubator of the most basic design for several years and invariably succeeds in hatching large numbers of this species every year. The hatchlings usually measure some 30mm SCL and weigh between 10-14g. Juveniles are roundish in overall shape, lacking both the elongate body form and flared marginals of the adults.

Malacochersus tornieri – **The Pancake Tortoise**

General: Malacochersus tornieri, the Pancake or Soft-shelled tortoise, is in many ways the most unusual tortoise in the world. It is certainly one which demonstrates a remarkable degree of adaption. Not only is it almost completely flat, but throughout life it remains soft and surprisingly flexible – a capability it employs to useful effect in defense by wedging itself in rocky fissures, expanding itself and thereby 'jamming' itself in very effectively. In order to effect this remarkable ability, the underlying bones are fenestrated. It is in addition rated as possibly the worlds fastest tortoise, and surprised specimens will usually run for cover rather than seek withdrawal into their shells for protection. Its distribution is limited to Kenya and Tanzania where it occurs in thorn covered rocky outcrops to an altitude in excess of 1600m.

Taxonomy: This tortoises taxonomy and nomenclature is not currently in dispute. There are no recognised sub-species.

Description: Both males and females are flat and entirely lack any evidence of the usual carapace 'dome'. Females are only marginally deeper in the body than males. The normally encountered maximum size of males is circa 167mm (height 36mm) whist that of females is 177mm (height 45mm). A male and female in our collection measure 160mm long by 34mm high and 170mm long by 43mm high respectively. The male weighs 360g and the female 550g. The ground colour of the carapace is typically a golden brown or horn colour with a distinct pattern of radiating black-brown marks. Females tend to have more of a rayed pattern than males which are characteristically more 'mottled' in appearance.

Captive environment: Pancake tortoises prefer a dry, rocky environment in captivity as they do in the wild. If a large, artificial 'mountain' can be provided with plenty of retreats and cracks then so much the better. These tortoises will spend hours scrambling over even the most precipitous terrain. Peak activity occurs in the morning and early evening, much of the day being spent in retreat under a convenient rocky ledge. They are inclined to be gregarious in habit, with several tortoises 'stacking' themselves on top of the other in a particularly favoured retreat. Two males placed together will however fight viciously during the breeding season, biting and snapping at each others heads and attempting to turn each other over. Their agility is such however that they can right themselves with little difficulty. Daytime temperatures should be in the order of 25–29° C although as is frequently the case with tortoises which inhabit high, dry places *Malacochersus tornieri* can

Malacochersus tornieri. The Pancake tortoise.

M. tornieri hatchling. Strangely, it does not look anything like as peculiar as adult specimens.

withstand considerably lower temperatures overnight. In captivity a minimum of 13° C is recommended. Damp is not much appreciated and should be avoided. This tortoise rarely drinks water, seemingly obtaining almost all of its fluid requirement from its food.

Diet: As for *G. pardalis* with a preference for grass and succulents. In captivity cabbage, lettuce, tomatoes and cucumber are taken readily. They seem little interested in most fruits, although melon is often an exception to this general rule. The diet should be supplemented as required with multi-vitamins and calcium – especially for egg laying females and juveniles.

Breeding: M. tornieri mate in a state of high excitement, the male vigorously snapping and biting at the females head and legs as he quickly and repeatedly circles her. Eggs are laid singly, and often at intervals of 6-8 weeks. A female in our own collection regularly produces such eggs which on average measures 47mm long by 31mm wide and weigh 35g. At 30°C incubated in a Type I container the incubation period is typically 140 days, but this does appear to be quite variable sometimes taking much longer. Incubation humidity should be medium to low. In the wild, eggs are laid in July or August, but the natural mean incubation period remains unknown. In captivity, females may choose to nest either during the daytime or early evening digging a fairly normal nest approximately 100mm in depth, or alternatively simply secreting the egg in a convenient nook or cranny among the rocks. Hatchlings upon emergence are strangely not particularly odd looking, and are even somewhat domed. Their profile is not dissimilar to that of *T. hermanni* for example. The hatchlings have a bright yellow groundcolour and plastron with deep brown-black spots on the vertebral and costal scutes. Typically newly emerged hatchlings measure about 40mm in length and weigh about 16-18g.

APPENDIX I

Values of Dietary Constituents and Additives

1. Calcium supplements

Some forms of calcium are more easily absorbed or utilised than others and some in themselves contain high levels of phosphorous. The best forms are those which have a high calcium percentage (Ca) and a low percentage of phosphorous (P). The approximate average Ca:P ratios of some commonly available additives are given below. From this it will be noted that calcium carbonate is a very good additive whilst calcium phosphate is a comparatively poor source.

	% Ca	% P
Calcium borogluconate	8.50	00.00
Calcium carbonate	40.00	00.00
Calcium gluconate	9.25	00.00
Calcium lactate	18.00	00.00
Calcium phosphate – monobasic	17.00	26.00
Calcium phosphate – dibasic	30.00	23.00
Calcium phosphate – tribasic	39.00	20.00
Standard bone mean	30.00	15.00

2. Nutritional analysis of natural foods

All figures are approximate averages – content varies seasonally. As most of the food items consumed in the wild by tortoises are not 'commercial' crops in many cases little or no data is available on their precise formulation.

Item	% protein	% fibre	% dry matter	% fat	% Ca	% P
Grass (winter)	4.00	37.00	40.00	1.00	0.75	0.06
Grass (summer)	6.00	n/a	n/a	2.00	0.35	0.20
Grass (lawn)	3.00	12.00	35.00	1.30	0.10	0.09
Forbs	9.00	n/a	n/a	2.75	1.80	0.40
Brome	8.50	31.00	35.00	1.00	0.28	0.23
Threeawn	6.30	35.00	n/a	1.50	0.60	0.09
Clover hay	11.00	30.00	n/a	1.90	1.00	0.20

3. Nutritional analysis of common substitute (captive) foods

All figures are approximate averages in grammes per 100g.

Item	Protein	Fibre	Fat	Ca (mg)	P (mg)	Vit-A (IU)
Apple	0.20	1.00	0.60	7.00	10.00	90.00
Aubergine	1.20	0.90	0.20	12.00	26.00	10.00
Avocado	2.20	1.50	17.00	10.00	42.00	290.00
Beet greens	2.20	1.30	3.00	119.00	40.00	6100.00
Broccoli	3.60	1.50	0.30	103.00	78.00	2500.00
Brussels Spouts	5.00	1.60	0.40	36.00	80.00	550.00
Cabbage	1.30	0.80	0.20	49.00	29.00	130.00
Carrot	1.10	1.00	0.20	37.00	36.00	1100.00
Cauliflower	2.70	1.00	0.20	25.00	56.00	60.00
Celeriac	1.80	1.30	0.30	43.00	115.00	00.00
Chicory greens	1.70	0.80	0.30	86.00	40.00	4000.00
Cucumber	0.90	0.60	0.10	25.00	27.00	250.00
Endive	1.70	0.90	0.10	81.00	54.00	3300.00
Fennel	2.80	0.50	0.40	100.00	51.00	3500.00
Lettuce	1.20	0.50	0.20	35.00	26.00	900.00
Lettuce, romaine	1.30	0.70	0.30	68.00	25.00	300.00
Lettuce, iceberg	0.90	0.50	0.10	20.00	22.00	1700.00
Peas, green	6.30	2.00	0.50	26.00	120.00	640.00
Peppers, sweet	1.20	1.40	0.22	9.00	22.00	420.00
Sprouting beans	3.80	0.70	0.20	19.00	64.00	20.00
Spinach	3.00	0.60	0.30	93.00	38.00	8100.00
Tomato	1.10	0.50	0.20	13.00	00.27	900.00
Turnip greens	3.00	0.80	0.90	246.00	58.00	7500.00
Watercress	2.20	0.70	0.30	151.00	55.00	4900.00

APPENDIX II

Viral agents, immunity and tortoises

The ecology of tortoises renders them potentially highly susceptible to viral diseases; they typically live an isolated existence in populations which are themselves isolated from others and which have probably remained isolated for thousands (sometimes tens of thousands) of years. As such, the opportunity to develop natural resistance to a wide range of organisms is severely limited. This of course applies equally to bacterial pathogens.

It should be recognised that even in the case of that most mobile of animals the human being, isolated populations are at increased risk from 'new' or alien organisms which may be introduced by visitors from populations where the same organism is endemic, but where acquired natural immunity has rendered it relatively harmless. A good example would be the common cold, which when introduced by early explorers decimated many previously isolated tribes in remote corners of the world. That example is well known, but what is not so well known is that current research indicates that even in a highly mobile and dense modern urban environment these effects are still present; epidemiologists hypothesise that some diseases including leukemias and cancers could result from "a rare response to an unidentified mild or sub-clinical infection which is facilitated when large numbers of people come together, particularly from a variety of origins"[1].

This is of direct relevance to the management of tortoises in captivity, which are often mixed together at random, with no thought to origins, in densities many hundreds of times greater than that which they experience in the wild. It is small wonder that mortality rates in large captive colonies tend to be so high, whereas an individual pet keeper with maybe one or two tortoises, purchased from the dealer at the same time (and hence usually from the same 'batch') and thereafter kept in isolation in the garden can often keep those same animals in good health for decades.

Certain species show greater sensitivity to infection than others; my own experience is that Gopher tortoises and north African tortoises are particularly sensitive. *Testudo ibera* and *T. hermanni* on the other hand seem relatively insensitive, as are *G. pardalis.* If tortoises of north African origin are placed in an overcrowded environment in close proximity to *T. ibera* or *T. ibera* or *T. hermanni*, then the rate of opportunistic disease incidence in the north African specimens rises dramatically. Typical problems include gut parasitism of flagellate origin, respiratory, ocular and mouth infections. Death is not uncommon. There are several possibilities which could explain this, but stress and an immune system unable to cope with 'alien' organisms must be a strongly suspected.

In the United States, a severe and often fatal respiratory disease has recently rampaged through wild populations of *Xerobates agassizi*; thousands of already endangered tortoises have so far died. In West Germany, a similarly mysterious disease has caused the deaths of many captive tortoises of a variety of species. In both cases viral organisms are either suspected or have already been identified[2].

It should be understood by everyone with responsibility for captive collections that the potential for an epidemical or genetic disaster is ever present. Under absolutely no circumstances should ex-captive animals simply be released into the wild. They could be carrying organisms which might spell death or even extinction for their species. I would also stress that animals which as part of an intended release program will eventually be released MUST NEVER be exposed to non-sympatric species from other geographical areas or even maintained in close proximity to them. Complete isolation must be maintained at all times.

In captive or zoo collections, a much improved survival rate (not to mention breeding success rate) will be noted if non-sympatric species are maintained separately and overcrowding is eliminated.

References:
[1] Kinlen, L. 1990. The Lancet, 7th Sept. 1990.
[2] Sachsse, W. 1990. Fatal epidemics from viral origins in tortoises. Lecture given to IVth Symposium Europeum Chelonologicum, Tuscany, Italy, 18–24 July 1990.

APPENDIX III

Useful addresses

The following specialist chelonian organisations can usually provide additional information on the captive care requirements of most species. Many publish regular newsletters or journals of interest to the tortoise and turtle enthusiast. Some organisations are mainly concerned with the turtle hobbyist, others are directly involved in tortoise or turtle conservation work. All offer useful information and access to expert advice. In addition to these specialist organisations, the national or regional general herpetological societies of most countries can usually provide technical advice on chelonians.

B.A.T.K,
c/o 323 Hagley Road,
Edgbaston,
Birmingham,
West Midlands,
B17 8ND,
England.

California Turtle and Tortoise Club,
P.O. Box 8952,
Fountain Valley,
California 92708,
U.S.A.

CARAPAX Project,
Centro Tartarughe,
C. P. 34,
58024 Massa Marittima,
Grosseto,
Italy.

Desert Tortoise Council,
P.O. Box 1738,
Palm Desert,
CA 92261,
U.S.A.

Desert Tortoise Preserve Committee,
P.O. Box 453,
Ridgecrest,
California,
CA 93556,
U.S.A.

Endangered Turtle Protection Foundation,
P.O. Box 417,
Greenville,
DE 18807,
U.S.A.

Gopher Tortoise Council,
611 N. W. 79th Drive,
Gainsville,
Florida,
FL 32607,
U.S.A.

Interessengemeinschaft Schildkroten Schutz,
Kelterbacherstr. 24,
D-5138 Heinsberg-Grebben,
West Germany.

Lubbock Turtle and Tortoise Society,
5/08 64th Street,
Lubbock,
Texas,
TX 79424,
U.S.A.

National Turtle and Tortoise Society Inc.,
P.O. Box 9806,
Phoenix,
Arizona,
AZ 85068-9806,
U.S.A.

New York Turtle and Tortoise Society,
163 Amsterdam Avenue,
Suite 365,
New York,
NY10023,
U.S.A.

Sacramento Turtle and Tortoise Club,
25 Starlit Circle,
Sacramento,
California,
CA 95831,
U.S.A.

San Diego Turtle and Tortoise Society,
13963 Lyons Valley Road,
Jamul,
California,
CA 92035-9607,
U.S.A.

S.O.P.I.O.M.,
Village des Tortues,
B.P. 24,
3590 Gonfaron,
France.

T.E.A.M.,
3245 Military Avenue,
Los Angeles,
CA 90034,
U.S.A.

The Tortoise Trust,
BM Tortoise,
London,
WC1N 3XX,
England

Tortoise Survival Project,
c/o The Tortoise Trust,
BM Tortoise,
London,
WC1N 3XX,
England.

TORT-Group,
5157 Poncho Circle,
Las Vegas,
Nevada 89119,
U.S.A.

Turtle Organisation of San Luis Obispo,
P.O. Box 3208,
Shell Beach,
CA 93449,
U.S.A.

Turtle and Tortoise Club of Santa Barbara,
P.O. Box 70745,
Santa Barbara,
CA 93160,
U.S.A.

GLOSSARY

Adaption – Morphological or behavioural modifications evolved over a period in response to environment or mode of life.

Aestivate – Summer or dry season dormancy. Not to be confused with hibernation.

Allantois – Sac-like growth surrounding an embryo. Assists with respiration and waste management.

Amnion – A fluid filed sac enclosing an embryo.

Anal – Pertaining to the anal region; e.g the anal suture of the plastron.

Anoxia – Lack of oxygen. Suffocation.

Anterior – Towards the front or head.

Aquatic – Living in water.

Areola – The central region of the scute. May be marked or raised.

Basking – Behaviour designed to gain maximum absorption of heat from the sun. Often involves positioning on slopes.

Beak – The horny outer covering of the jaws.

Bimodality – The term used to describe non simultaneous hatching.

Bioclimatic range – The forces of temperature and humidity among other factors which influence distribution of a species.

Body temperature – The interior rather than exterior surface temperature of the body. Usually measured per cloaca.

Carapace – The hard bony upper shell of the tortoise or turtle.

Carnivore – An animal which eats the flesh of other animals. Not common in tortoises but frequent in freshwater turtles. e.g. Snapping turtles.

Caudal – Pertaining to the tail region.

Character – Any key feature used to diagnose species or sex.

Chelonian – A shield reptile. Tortoises, turtles and terrapins.

Circum Mediterranean – From around the Mediterranean sea.

Cline – A gradual morphological variation within a species from one part of its range to another.

Cloaca – The chamber and vent in the tail.

Clutch – The collective term for all the eggs laid by a female at one time.

Clutch density – The number of eggs in a single clutch.

Contiguous – A sequential or unbroken series or distribution.

Coprophagous – Dung or faeces eating.

Costal – The series of plates located at the side and middle of a chelonians shell between the vertebrals and marginals.

Cranial – Pertaining to the skull.

Cutaneous – Of or pertaining to the skin.

Dimorphism – Two distinct forms within a species. Sexual dimorphism is the existence of morphological divergence between male and female.

Diurnal – Active during the day.

Dorsal – Pertaining to the upper part.

127

Dystocia – See egg-binding.

ESD – Acronym for Environmental Sex Determination.

Ecosystem – The natural symmetry between organisms and their environment.

Ectoparasite – A parasite that lives outside the body or on its surface.

Ectotherm – An organism which mainly relies upon environmental sources to sustain its body temperature.

Egg binding – A condition which occurs in female tortoises involving difficulty in laying eggs (Dystocia).

Egg caruncle – A small projection on the beak of hatchlings used for the purposes of piercing the egg.

Egg tooth – See egg caruncle.

Endemic – Zoogeographically restricted species, race or form.

Endoparasite – An internal parasite, e.g a 'worm'.

Endotherm – An animal which self-generates heat by metabolic action, e.g. a mammal.

Exotherm – See ectotherm.

FSL – Acronym for Full Spectrum Lighting, 'artificial sunlight'.

Family – The taxonomic category below Order and above Genus.

Fauna – The animal life of a locality.

Fenestrated – Pierced. With gaps or holes.

Form – A population or 'variety'; not necessarily deserving of separate systematic recognition but also sometimes denoting a true species or subspecies.

Genetic – Pertaining to genes and inheritance.

Genus – The taxonomic category below Family and above Species. Contains one or more species.

Gestation – In tortoises, the period between fertilisation of an egg and laying.

Gregarious – Tending to congregate in groups.

Gular – Pertaining to the throat region; in tortoises usually refers to the plastral scutes below the head.

Gut – The alimentary canal, especially the intestine.

Habitat – The environment in which an animal lives.

Hatchling – The young animal just after it leaves the egg; any juvenile phase tortoise to about 6 months.

Hepatic – Pertaining to the liver.

Herbivore – An animal which eats plants rather than other animals. A vegetarian.

Herpetology – The science and study of reptiles and amphibians.

Hibernation – Winter dormancy characterised by specific biological and biochemical changes including lowered blood pressure and respiration rate.

Hinge – A mobile suture; as seen in Box Turtles or Hinge-back tortoises which allows part of the shell to be closed.

Homogenous – A relatively intact distribution of genetic material within a population. Little diversity from one locality to another within the range.

Hybrid – An individual resulting from a mating of parents which are not genetically identical, e.g which belong to different species.

Incubation – The developmental phase of an egg prior to hatching which requires warmth.

Infrared – Invisible heat rays beyond the visible light spectrum.

Intergrade – A hybrid form.

Introduced – A species not native to a region but which now occur there as a result of artificial transport or escapes from captivity etc.

Introflexed – Turned inwards.

Juvenile – Not sexually mature.

Keel – A ridge sometimes seen in the vertebral region of the carapace.

Keratin – A tough fibrous protein present in epidermal structures such as carapace shields, beaks and claws.

Kinesis – Mobile. As in a Box Turtle or Hinge-back shell.

Lateral – Pertaining to the side.

Marginal – The series of smaller scutes at the very edge of the carapace. Usually 11 on each side in most species.

Melanistic – Darker or blacker than normal.

Mesic – An intermediate humidity habitat.

Metabolic rate – The rate of energy expenditure by an organism.

Metabolism – The chemical or energy changes which occur within an animal necessary to sustain life.

Microclimate – The climate immediately surrounding an animal. May differ profoundly from the general climate in the case of burrowing tortoises.

Morphology – Pertaining to shape and form.

Morphometry – The technique of measuring and comparing shapes, e.g. the shape of a turtle shell.

Myelitis – Tissue destruction due to infection.

Nares – Paired openings of the nasal cavity.

Nasal – Pertaining to the nose or nares.

Nocturnal – Active at night.

Nuchal – A small scute at the front of the carapace, above the head.

Oedema – Fluid retention. Can signify renal disease or bruising. Any swelling.

Omnivore – An animal which feeds on both plant and animal tissue.

Optic – Pertaining to the eyes.

Osteological – Pertaining to the bones and their stucture.

Oviposition – The act of egg laying.

P.O. – Preferred Optimum.

Parenteral – Via injection.

Phenetic – Apparent similarity on the basis of external characters.

Phylogeny – Pertaining to evolutionary relationships.

Plastron – The lower surface of the chelonian shell.

Poikilotherm – See ectotherm.

Population – A group of the same species living in a discreet geographical area.

Posterior – The rear or back part.

Race – A population of a species distinguishable from the rest of that species. A subspecies.

Radial – Like the spokes of a wheel.

Renal – Pertaining to the kidneys.

Savannah – A habitat of open plains and low grassy vegetation.

SCL – Acronym for Straight Carapace Length (not over the curve).

Scute – The horny plates of a chelonian shell.

Serrated – Jagged or saw-like.

Subspecies – A subdivision of a single species given a unique name which is expressed after the generic and species name. See race.

Substrate – In herpetology, usually refers to vivarium flooring material.

Supra – Pertaining to above.

Supracaudal – The scute above the tail.

Sutures – The 'seams' between two boney or horny plates.

Sympatric – Living in the same geographical area.

Synonym – One of several different names applied to an identical taxonomic category only one of which is valid. The invalid names only are called synonyms. The valid name is selected by priority.

Systemic – Whole body treatment. Not topical. Usually by injection.

Taxon – A taxonomic category, e.g a Family, Genus or Species.

Taxonomy – The science of classification.

Temperate – Latitudes where summer and winter seasons are experienced.

Terrapin – In this work, applied to fresh water aquatic chelonians.

Terrestrial – Living on the ground. Not Aquatic.

Topically – Pertaining to surface application.

Tortoise – In this work, applied to exclusively terrestrial chelonians.

Tropical – Pertaining to equatorial regions where winter and summer seasons are not experienced.

Tubercle – The 'spur' on a tortoises thighs.

Turtle – In this work, applied to semi-terrestrial chelonians and marine chelonians. Sometimes applied interchangeably with 'tortoise'.

Tympanitic – Pertaining to the ear.

Type – The original specimen upon which a species is erected.

Type locality – The place where the Type was collected or originated.

Ventral – Pertaining to the underside.

Vertebral – Pertaining to the spinal region. The central row of scutes along the top of the carapace.

Vivarium – An indoor artificial environment containing animals.

Xiphiplastra – The rearmost pair of plastral bones.

Zoogeography – The science of animal distribution.

SELECT BIBLIOGRAPHY AND FURTHER READING
(arranged by genus)

Geochelone

Anonymous. 1988. Yellowfoot and Redfoot tortoises: *Geochelone denticulata* and *Geochelone carbonaria*. T.E.A.M. 1(5): 2-4.

Archer, W.H. 1948. The mountain tortoise (*G. pardalis*). Afr. Wildlife. 2(3): 74-79.

Bacon, J.P. 1980. Some observations on the captive management of Galapagos tortoises. **In** *Reproductive Biology and Diseases of Captive Reptiles* (eds. Murphy, J.B. and Collins, J.T.). SSAR.

Bartlett, R.D. 1982. An incidence of twinning in the Malagassy tortoise, *Geochelone radiata*. Tortuga Gazette, April 1982: 4.

Beltz, R.E. 1968. A world tour of the *Geochelone*. Int. Turtle Tortoise Soc. J. 2(1): 12-17, 27-29.

Bennefield, B.L. 1982. Captive breeding of the tropical Leopard tortoise *Geochelone pardalis babcocki* in Zimbabwe. Testudo 2(1): 1-5.

Bowker, F. 1926. Tortoise eggs and nests. S. Af. J. Nat. Hist. 6: 37.

Boycott, R.C. and Bourquin, O. 1988. The South African Tortoise Book. Southern Book Publishers, Johannesburg.

Censky, E.J. 1988. *Geochelone carbonaria* (Reptilia: Testudines) in the West Indies. Fla. Sci. 51(2): 108-114.

Coakley, J. and Klemens, M. 1983. Two generations of captive-hatched Leopard tortoises *Geochelone pardalis babcocki*. Herp Review 14(2): 43-44.

Coles, R.W. 1985. Reproductive data: the Leopard tortoise (*Geochelone pardalis*). Herptile, 10(1): 28-29.

Daniel, J.C. 1983. The Book of Indian Reptiles. Bombay.

Davis, S. 1979. Husbandry and breeding of the Red-footed tortoise *Geochelone carbonaria* at the National Zoological Park, Washington. Int. Zoo Yearbook, pp. 50-53. London, England.

Flint, M. 1977. Captive husbandry and reproduction of the Leopard tortoise *Geochelone pardalis babcocki*. Proc. 2nd. An. Reptile Symp. on Captive Propagation and Husbandry. pp. 113-119.

Hine, M.L. 1980. Reproduction of the Leopard Tortoise in captivity. Testudo. 1(3): 40-43.

Jakob, R. 1970. Notes on keeping and rearing the Jaboty tortoise *Testudo denticulatta*. Rep. Jersey. Wild. Pres. Trust. 7: 49050.

Klemens, M. 1974. Captive breeding of the Leopard tortoise (*Geochelone pardalis*). Conn. Herp. Soc. Bull. 5: 5-7.

Legler, J.M. 1963 Tortoises (*Geochelone carbonaria*) in Panama: distribution and variation. American Midland Naturalist, 70(2): 490-503.

May, C.D. 1983. Some tips for choosing breeder tortoises (*G. carbonaria*). Notes from NOAH, 10(12).

Moll, D. and Tucker, J.K. 1976. Growth and maturity of the red-footed tortoise *Geochelone carbonaria*. Bull. Md. Herpet. Soc. 12(3): 96-98.

Mowbray, L.S. 1966. A note on breeding South American tortoises Testudo denticulata at Bermuda Zoo. Int. Zoo. Yearbook. 6: 216.

Pritchard, P.C.H. and Trebbau, P. 1984. The Turtles of Venezuela. SSAR. Ohio.

Rowe, J. and Janulaw, J. 1980. A noteworthy conservation achievement Chelonologica, 1(3): 125-131.

Shaw, C.E. 1967. Breeding the Galapagos tortoise – success story. Oryx 9(2): 119-130.

Vokins, A.M.A. 1977. Breeding the red foot tortoise *Geochelone carbonaria* (Spix 1824). Dodom 14: 73-80.

Wilson, V.J. 1968. The Leopard tortoise *Testudo pardalis babcocki* in eastern Zambia. Arnoldia Rhodesia, 3: 1-11.

Gopherus and Xerobates

Anonymous. 1981. Care of adult tortoises. Tortuga Gazette, July 1981: 3-6.

Anonymous. 1983. Care of California and Texas Desert tortoise hatchlings. Tortuga Gazette, July 1983. pp. 7-9.

Anonymous. 1985. How to adopt and care for Desert tortoises. Tort-Group, Nevada.

Appleton, A. 1985. Breeding the Bolson tortoise. Tortuga Gazette, Feb. 1985: 6-7.

Arata, A.A. 1958. Notes on the eggs and young of *Gopherus polyphemus* (Daudin). Quart. Journ. Florida. Acad. Sci. 21: 274-280.

Auffenberg, W. 1976. The Genus *Gopherus* (Testudinidae): 1. Osteology and Relationships of extant Species. Bull. Florida State Museum. 20(2): 47-110.

Berry, Kristin. 1990. Commonly asked questions about the Desert tortoise and answers. Tortoise Tracks, 11(1).

Bour, R. and Dubois, A. 1984. *Xerobates:* a synonym older than *Scraptochelys*. Bull. Mens. Soc. Linn. Lyon. 53(1): 30-32.

Bramble, D.M. 1982. *Scraptochelys*: Generic division and evolution of gopher tortoises. Copeia 1984(4): 862–867.

Brame, A.H. and Peerson, D.J. 1969. Tortoise ID. Int. Tortoise and Turtle. Soc. J. Sept-Oct. 1969. pp. 8-12.

Brown, D.A. 1965. Nesting of captive *Gopherus berlandieri* (Agassiz). Herpetologica, 15: 101–102.

Connor, M.J. 1989. Molecular biology and the Turtle; the Desert tortoise and its relatives. Tortuga Gazette, 25(8): 10-11.

Fowler, M.E. 1980. Comparison of respiratory infection and hypovitaminosis-A in Desert tortoises. Comparative Pathology in Zoo Animals, Washington.

Hansen, R.M., Johnson, M.K. and Van Devender, T.R. 1976. Foods of the Desert tortoise *Gopherus agassizi* in Arizona and Utah. Herpetologica 32: 247-251.

Iverson, J.B. 1980. The reproductive biology of *Gopherus polyphemus* Chelonia Testudinidae. Am. Midland Nat. 103(2): 353–359.

Jackson, G. and Trotter, J.A., T.H. and M.W. 1976. Accelerated growth rate and early maturity in *Gopherus agassizi*. Herpetologica 32: 139-145.

Kirchman, V. 1976. Gopherus Tortoise Care Sheets. San Diego Turtle and Tortoise Soc. pp. 6.

Lamb, T., Avise, J.C. and Gibbons, J.W. 1989. Phylogeographic patterns in mitochondrial DNA of the desert tortoise (*Xerobates agassizi*) and evolutionary relationships among the North American gopher tortoises. Evolution, 43: 76-87.

Lee, H.H. 1964. Egg laying in captivity by *Gopherus agassisi*. Herpetologica 19: 62–65.

Legler, J.M. 1959. A new tortoise, genus *Gopherus*, from Northcentral Mexico. Univ. Kansas. Pub. Mus. Nat. Hist. II: 335–343.

McGinnis, S.M. and Voight, W.G. 1971. Thermoregulation in the Desert tortoise, *Gopherus agassizi*. Comp. Biochem. Physiol. 40A: 119-126.

Nichols, U.G. 1957. The desert tortoise in captivity. Herpetologica 13: 141-144.

Poorman, F. & R. 1971. *agassizi* Vs. *berlandieri*. Int. Tortoise and Turtle Soc. J. Jan–Feb. 1971: 14–16.

Rosskopf, W.J. 1981. Initial three year mortality study on Desert tortoises. Tortuga Gazette, May 1981. pp. 4-5.

Trotter, J. 1973. Incubation made easy. Int. Turtle and Tortoise Soc. J. Jan–Feb 1973. pp. 26–31.

Kinixys
Archer, W.H. 1968. The Tortoise with a difference. Int. Turtle Tortoise Soc. J. 2(4): 11–13, 35–36.

Broadley, D.G. 1981. A review of the populations of *Kinixys* (Testudinidae) occurring in south-eastern Africa. Ann. Cape. Prov. Mus. 13: 195-216.

Highfield, A.C. 1989. *Kinixys belliana*. The Carapace. 5(5): 9-10.

Kuchling, G. 1986. Biology of *Kinixys belliana* at Nosy Faly, Madagascar. **in**: *Studies in Herpetology* (ed. Rocek, Z.). Charles U.P., Prague. pp. 435-440.

Kuchling, G. 1989. Okologie, Lebensweise und Uberlebenchancen der Landschildkroten Madagaskars. Salamandra. 25(3/4): 169-190.

Laurent, R.F. 1962. On the races of *Kinixys belliana* Gray. Breviora, Mus. Comp. Zool. 176: 1-6.

Pond, S. and L. 1989. Experiences with captive breeding of the African Hinge-back tortoise, *Kinixys belliana*. Plastron Papers, XIX (2): 12-14.

Sachsse, W. 1980. Zur biologie und Fortpflanzung von *Kinixys belliana nogueyi*. Salamandra 16.

Villiers, A. 1958. tortues et crocodiles de L'Afrique Noire Francaise. I.F.A.N., Dakar. pp. 1-354.

Malacochersus

Eglis, A. 1960. Notes on the Soft-shell tortoise *Malacochersus tornieri* (Siebenrock). Herpetologica 16: 12-14.

Eglis, A. 1964. Flat and fast – the Pancake tortoise. Animal. Kingd. 68: 107-110.

Juvik, J.O. 1971. Chimney climber. Int. Turtle Tortoise Soc. J. 1(2): 29, 44-45.

Shaw, C.E. 1970. The hardy (and prolific) Soft-shelled tortoise. Int. Tortoise and Turtle Soc. J. Jan–Feb 1970: 6-31.

Terrapene

Allard, H.A. 1935. The natural history of the Box turtle. Sci. Monthly, 41: 325-338.

Allard, H.A. 1948. The eastern Box turtle and its behaviour. J. Tennessee Acad. Sci. 23: 307-321.

Anonymous. 1989. Caring for your Box turtle. Voice of the Turtle, 18(10): 5-6.

Beaman, K.R. 1989. Turtle of the Month: Common Box turtle *Terrapene carolina*. Tortuga Gazette, 25(11): 3-4.

Beezley, C. 1969. Gentle Hermit. Texas Parks and Wildlife. XXVII(4).

Behler, J.L. and King F.W. 1979. The Audubon Society Field Guide to North American reptiles and amphibians. A. Knopf, New York.

Carpenter, C.C. 1957. Hiberntion, Hibernacula and associated behaviour of the Three-toed Box turtle (*Terrapene carolina triunguis*). Copeia, 4: 278-282.

Cohen, H.J. 1977. Breeding Report: *Terrapene carolina carolina*. Chelonia, 3(3): 5.

Conant, R. 1975. A Field Guide to the reptiles and amphibians of eastern and central North America. Houghton Mifflin, Boston.

Ditmars, R.L. 1934. A review of the Box turtles. Zoologica (N.Y.) 17: 1–44.

Englehardt, G.P. 1916. Burrowing habits of the Box turtle. Copeia, 1916: 42–43.

Labrecque, J. 1982. Turtle of the Month: The American Box turtle. Tortuga Gazette, August 1982. 5–8.

Legler, J.M. 1960. Natural history of the ornate Box turtles *Terrapene ornata ornata* Agassiz. Univ. Kansas. Publ. Mus. Nat. Hist. 11: 527–669.

Marquard, K.H. 1988. Bericht aus dem Alltag zweir Dreizehen Dosenschildkroten (*Terrapene carolina triunguis*). De Schildkrote 2(2): 32–36.

Metcalf, E. and Metcalf, A.L. 1970. Observations on ornate Box turtles (*Terrapene ornata ornata* Agassiz). Kansas Acad. Sci. Trans. 73(1): 96–117.

Penn, G.H. and Pottharst, K.E. 1940. The reproduction and dormancy of *Terrapene c. carolina* in New Orleans. Herpetologica, 2: 25–29.

Pope, C.H. 1949. Turtles of the United States and Canada. Knopf, N.Y.

Stettler, P.H. 1990. Experiences with Box turtles. Reptile Keeper International 1(5): 17–18.

Whetmore, A. 1920. Observations on the hibernation of Box turtles. Copeia, 77: 3–5.

Testudo

Anderson, S.C. 1979. Synopsis of the turtles, crocodiles and amphisbaeans of Iran. Proc. Calif. Acad. Sci. 41(22): 501–528.

Andreu, A.C. and Villamore, M.D. 1986. Reproduction of *Testudo graeca graeca* in Donana, SW Spain. In Studies in Herpetology, Prague. ed. Rocek. pp. 589–592.

Bour, R. 1987. L'identite' des Tortues terrestres europenes: specimens-types et localities-types. Revue fr. Aquariol., 13 (1986) pp. 111–122.

Bour, R. 1989. Caracteres diagnostiques offerts par le crane des tortues terrestres du genre *Testudo*. Mesogee 48: 13–19.

Bruekers, J.M.B.M. 1986. Schildpadden in Zuid-Frankrijk. Lacerta (44): 4 63–65.

Brushko, Z.K. and Kubykin, R.A. 1977. Data of reproduction of the Steppe tortoise in the Southern Balkhash Lake region. Proc. Zoo. Inst. Acad. Sci. UUSR. 74: 32–34.

Buskirk, J. 1967. Turtles of the Holy Land. Int. Turtle Tortoise Soc. J. 1: 20–23.

Cheylan, M. 1981. Biologie et Ecologie de la tortue d'Hermann *Testudo hermanni* GMELIN 1789. Mem. Trav. E.P.H.E. Inst. Montpellier (13): 1-404.

Collins, P.W.P. 1980. The Captive Breeding of Mediterranean tortoises in Britain. **In**. British. Herp. Soc.: *Care and Breeding of Captive Reptiles.* pp. 21-36.

Devaux, B. 1988. La Tortue Sauvage. Sang de la terre, Paris.

Dickinson, P. 1985. Maintenance, behaviour and breeding of African Spur-thighed Tortoise. Int. Zoo News No. 194. 32(6): 3-19.

Hempel, Wolfgang. 1988. Haltung und Nachzucht bei *Agrionemys horsfieldi*. De Schildkrote 2(2): 12-19.

Highfield, A.C. 1986. Safer Hibernation & Your Tortoise. Tortoise Trust, 28pp, reprinted as serial in The Carapace, NL of Nat. Turtle & Tortoise Society, Inc. Phoenix, Arizona. 1989.

Highfield, A.C. 1987. Causal Factors of Mortality in Captive Collections. Lecture at University of Bristol Symposium. Published in Testudo, 2(5).

Highfield, A.C. 1988. A new size record for *T. hermanni* GMELIN 1789?. The Rephiberary 132: 5-6.

Highfield, A.C. 1989. Terrestrial Chelonia; Incubation of Eggs & Care of Hatchlings. The Tortoise Trust, London. 29pp.

Highfield, A.C. 1989. Embryonic anoxia and the incubation of turtle eggs. Plastron Papers. Vol. XIX No. 2. p. 31.

Highfield, A.C. 1989. Diagnostic characters of Tortoises (1): Division of the Supracaudal scute in *Testudo* and its relevance as a taxonomic Diagnostic Character. British Herpetological Society Bulletin. 30: 14-18.

Highfield, A.C. 1989. Artificial incubation techniques in relation to *Testudo graeca* and *T. hermanni* with notes on Embryonic Anoxia as a possible factor in hatchling mortality in captive breeding programs. Voice of the Turtle 18(12), San Diego, CA.

Highfield, A.C. 1989. Feeding your tortoise. Tortoise Trust, London.

Highfield, A.C. 1989. General care of tortoises. Tortoise Trust, London.

Highfield, A.C. 1989. Revision of Taxonomic Status and Nomenclature; Genus *Testudo*; A brief chronology. The Rephiberary nr. 141.

Highfield, A.C. 1989. 200 years of Tortoise Taxonomy. The Rephibiary. ASRA Newsletter No. 145.

Highfield, A.C. 1989 Tortoise Survival Project. Voice of the Turtle, San Diego Tortoise & Turtle Society. 18:(11).

Highfield, A.C. 1990. New record size for North African *Testudo*. British Herpetological Soc. Bulletin. 31: 29-30.

Highfield, A.C. 1990. Preliminary report on the Taxonomic, Biotypic and Conservation status of the Land Tortoises of Tunisia. Tortoise Survival Project, London.

139

Highfield, A.C. (in press) Biotype, nomenclature and taxonomic diagnostic characters of *Testudo hermanni hermanni* GMELIN 1789 in Southern France with preliminary notes on comparative egg morphology with *T. h. boettgeri* MOJSISOVICS 1889.

Highfield, A.C. (in press) Diagnostic characters of Tortoises (2): Studies in the Comparative Morphology of the eggs of Tortoises, genus *Testudo* and their relevance as Characters in Diagnostic Taxonomy.

Highfield, A.C. & Martin, J. 1989 A Revision of the Testudines of North Africa, Asia and Europe, Genus: *Testudo*. J. Chel. Herp. (1): 11-12.

Highfield, A.C. & Martin, J. 1989 *Testudo whitei* BENNETT 1836; New light on an old carapace – Gilbert White's Selborne tortoise re-discovered. Journal of Chelonian Herpetology (1):1 13-22.

Highfield, A.C. & Martin, J. 1989. An introduction to a conservation project for the North African tortoise, including a description of *Testudo flavominimaralis*, n.species. Tortoise Trust, London.

Highfield, A.C. & Martin, J. (in press). The true Status and diagnosis of *Testudo terrestris* FORSKAL 1775 with additional notes upon the status and nomenclature of *Testudo floweri* BODENHEIMER 1935.

Hine, M.L. 1982. Notes on the Marginated tortoise (*Testudo marginata*) in Greece and in Captivity. Bull. Brit. Herpet. Soc. No. 5.

Khozatsky, L.I and Mlynarski, M. 1966. *Agrionemys* – nouveau genre de tortues terrestres (Testudinidae). Bull. Ac. Polon. Sci. (2): 123-125.

Kirsche, W. 1979. The housing and regular breeding of Mediterranean tortoises *Testudo* spp. in captivity. Int. Zoo Yearbook, 19: 42-49.

Lambert, M.R.K. 1981. Temperature, activity & field sighting in the Mediterranean spur-thighed or common garden tortoise tortoise *Testudo graeca* L. Biological Conservation. (21): 39-54.

Lambert, M.R.K. 1982. Studies on the growth, structure and abundance of the Mediterranean spur-thighed tortoise, *Testudo graeca* in field populations. J. Zool. Soc. London, 196: 165-189.

Lambert, M.R.K. 1988. Natural bioclimatic range and the growth of captive-bred Mediterranean *Testudo* L. in northern Europe: Implications for conservation farming. B.H.S. Bulletin, 24: 6-7.

Loveridge, A. and Williams, E.E. 1957. Revision of the African tortoises and turtles of the suborder Cryptodira. Bull. Mus. Comp. Zool. Harv. Coll. 115: 163-557.

Madge, D. 1985. Temperature and sex determination in reptiles with reference to Chelonia. Testudo 2(3): 8-13.

Mertens, R. 1946. Uber einige mediterrane Schildkrotenrassen. Senckenbergiana Biol. 27: 111-118.

Obst, F.J. and Meusel, W. 1969. Die Landschildkroten Europas. Die Neue Brehm- Bucherei. Wittenberg-Lutherstadt.

Pelaz, M.P. 1988. Aspectos historicos para la actual corologia de *Testudo hermanni* en la Mediterraneo Occidental. Vida Silvestre nr. 64 (ICONA - Madrid) 28-25.

Terent'ev, P.V. and Chernov, S.A. 1965. Key to the Amphibians and Reptiles. 3rd ed. Prog. Sci. Trans. Jerusalem, Israel.

Wermuth, H. 1952. *Testudo hermanni robertmertensi* n. subsp. und ihr Vorkommen in Spanien. Senckenbergiana, 33: 157-164.

Wermuth, H. 1958. Status und nomenklatur der maurischen land-schildkrote, *Testudo graeca*, in S. W. Asien and N. O. Africa. Senck. Biol. 39: 149-153.

Miscellaneous

Anonymous. 1961. Tortoise growth. Zoonooz 34(1): 12.

Adams, J.W. 1989. A plague upon a turtle's house: "Shell Rot" or ulcerative shell disease. Plastron Papers, XVIII. No. 7: 17-18.

Avery, R.A. 1986. The physiology of reproduction. Testudo 2(4): 8-13.

Bellairs, A. 1969. The Life of Reptiles (2 Vols.). Weidenfeld and Nicholson, London.

Bellairs, A. and Cox, C.B. (eds) 1976. Morphology and Biology of Reptiles. Academic Press, London.

Boyer, D.R. 1965. Ecology of the basking habit in turtles. Ecology, 46: 99-113.

Branch, Bill. 1988. Field guide to the snakes and other reptiles of Southern Africa. New Holland Publishers, London.

Brattstrom, B.H. and Collins, R. 1972. Thermoregulation. Int. Tortoise and Turtle Soc. J. 6(5): 15-19.

Bull, J.J. 1980. Sex determination in reptiles. Quart. Rev. Biol. 55: 3-21.

Carr, A. 1952. Handbook of Turtles. Cornell U. P. New York.

Congdon, J.D. and Gibbons, J.W. 1985. Egg components and reproductive characteristics of turtles: relationships to body size. Herpetologica 41(2): 194-205.

Cooper, J.E. and Jackson, O.F. 1981. Diseases of the Reptilia. Academic Press, London.

Ernst, C.H. and Barbour, R.W. 1972. Turtles of the United States. U.P. Kentucky.

Frye, F. 1973. Husbandry, Medicine and Surgery in Captive Reptiles. V.M. Publications, Kansas.

Frye, F. 1974. The role of nutrition in the successful maintenance of captive reptiles. Cal. Vet. Med. Assn. 86th Ann. Seminar. Sylabus. pp. 5-15.

Frye, F. 1981. Biomedical and Surgical aspects of captive reptile husbandry. V. M. Publications, Kansas.

Gans, C. (ed.) 1969 onwards in 13 Vols. Biology of the Reptilia. Academic Press, London.

Groombridge, B. 1982 The IUCN Amphibia-Reptilia Red Data Book part 1. IUCN, Switzerland.

Harless, M. and Morlock, H. (eds) 1979. Turtles: Perspectives and Research. John Wiley and Sons, New York.

Highfield, A.C. 1987. Electronic temperature Measurement and Control for Incubators and Vivaria. The Herptile. Journ. International. Herpet. Soc. Vol. 12(4): 130-133.

Highfield, A.C. 1988. Husbandry Notes; Observations on Dehydration in Reptiles. The Rephiberary, nr. 130.

Highfield, A.C. 1988. Husbandry Notes; Force-feeding chelonians – supportive therapy techniques. The Rephiberary, nr. 131.

Highfield, A.c. 1989. Flagellate & Ciliate Protozoan infections in Tortoises. The Herptile, 14(1): 4-8.

Highfield, A.C. 1989. Notes on dietary constituents for Herbivorous terrestrial chelonia and their effects on Growth and Development. ASRA (U.K.) Journal, Vol. 3 (3): 7-20.

Inskeep, R. 1983. Incubator construction. Testudo, 2(2): 40-42.

Iverson, J.B. 1986. A checklist with distribution maps of the Turtles of the World. Richmond, Indiana.

Kaplan, H.M. 1957. The care and diseases of laboratory turtles. Proc. Anim. Care Panel. 7: 259-272.

Keymer, J.F. 1978. Diseases of chelonians: (1) Necropsy survey of tortoises. Vet. Record. 103: 548-552.

Lawrence, K. 1983. The treatment of disease in reptiles. ASRA (U.K.) J. 2(2): 18-25.

Lawrence, K. and Needham, J.R. 1985. Rhinitis in long term captive Mediterranean tortoises (*Testudo graeca* and *Testudo hermanni*). Vet. Record. 117: 662-664.

Marcus, L. 1981. Veterinary biology and medicine of captive amphibians and reptiles. Lea and Febiger, Philadelphia.

Millichamp, N.J. 1980. **In**: *The Care and Breeding of Captive Reptiles*. BHS, London.

Murphy, J.B. n.d. A Brief outline of suggested treatments for diseases of captive reptiles. SSAR and Kansas Herpet. Soc.

Murphy, J.B. 1973. A review of diseases and treatment of captive chelonians. HISS News-Journal. 1(1): 5-8.

Obst, F.J. 1986. Turtles, Tortoises and Terrapins. Macmillan of Australia, Melbourne.

Pfeiffer, C. 1980. Foods for Tortoises. Chelonologica, 1:(1): 5-13.

Pritchard, P.C.H. 1979. Encyclopedia of Turtles. TFH, New Jersey.

Ross, Richard A. 1984. The Bacterial diseases of Reptiles. Institute for Herpetological Research, California.

Smith, R.N. 1985. The tortoise egg. Testudo 2(3): 7.

Tryon, B. 1975. How to incubate reptile eggs: a proven technique. Bull. N.Y. Herp. Assoc. 11(3-4): 33-37.

Yntema, C.L. 1976. Effects of incubation temperature on sexual differentiation in the turtle *Chelydra serpentina*. J. Morphol. 150(2): 453–462.

Wallach, J. 1969. Medical care of reptiles. J. Am. Vet. Assn. 155: 1017–1034.

Wallach, J. 1971. Environmental and nutritional diseases of captive reptiles. J. Am. Vet. Assn. 159(11): 1632–1643.

Young, J.D. 1950. The structure and some physical properties of the testudian eggshell. Proc. Zool. Soc. Lond. 120: 455–469.

Zimmermann, E. 1986. Breeding terrarium animals. TFH, N.J.

Zwart, P. 1987. Advances in the veterinary care of chelonians over the past 20 years (1967–1987). Testudo 2(5): 1–14.

Zwart, P. and Truyens, E.H.A. 1975. Hexamitiasis in tortoises. Vet. Parasitology. 1: 175–183.

INDEX

Marginated tortoise, see *Testudo marginata*
Membranes, embryonic, 12-15
Mesoderm, 15
Metaplasia, 42
Methionine, 69
Metronidazole, 56, 58
Mexican tortoise, 2, 82
Microscope, 54, 55, 58
Mites, 53
Mouth rot, see Necrotic Stomatitis
Mucous, excess, 66
Mycoses, 59, 67

Nares, infected, 66
Nasal antibiotics, 67
Necrotic stomatitis, 60-62
Nematodes, 54-56
Neomycin, 62
Nephritis, 58
Nest sites, selection of, 15, 16
Niclosamide, 56
Nomenclature, taxonomic, 5
North african tortoises, 2-3, 108-111
- susceptibility to infection, 121
Nystatin, 59

Oedema, 68
Organisations, tortoise, 122-125
Ornate Box turtle, 86-90
Oropharyngeal culture, 66
Osteodystrophy, 44-46
Osteogenesis, 14
Osteomyelitis, 61
Osteoporosis, 45, 47
Overwintering, 39, 89, 107
Oxfendazole, 54-55
Oxygen, requirement in incubation, 13
Oxytetracycline, 63, 64, 67, 68
- doses, 65, 70
Oxytocin, 68, 85
Oxyurids, 54
Panacur, see fenbendazole
Parasites, 53-59, 92
Peritonitis, 55, 67
- egg, 68
Petechiation, 67

Phenothiazine, 54
Plastron, 6, 9, 8, 27, 67, 78, 86, 91, 112-113
- dimorphism of, 6-9
- of hatchling, 27
- haemorrhage under, 67
Pancake tortoise, see *M. tornieri*
Pet foods, 42, 47, 64, 89
- canned, 42
- fat content, 42, 89
- and diseases, 64
Phosphate, relative values, 118-119
Piperazine, 54
Pneumonia, 65-66
Predation, 2, 3, 9
Proportional thermostats, 20
Protein, dietary, 49-51
Protozoan, organisms, 56-58
Pyxidea, 86

Radiology, 40
Rain, as breeding initiator, 95
- as hatching initiator, 25-26, 101
- induces activity, 88, 95
Red-foot tortoise, see *G. carbonaria*
Renal disease, 42, 57, 58, 68-69
Renal system, 48, 68-69
Resistance, disease, 69, 120-121
Respiratory diseases, 65-67
Retraction, poor, 66
Rhinitis, 66-67
Rhinoclemys, 86
Runny nose, see Rhinitis

Salmonella, 71
Salt basin Box turtle, 86-90
Sand, 22
Scour, digestive, 56-57
Scutes, deformed, 50-51
Sensitivity, antibiotic, 61
Septicaemia, 67-68
Sexual dimorphism, 7, 8, 9
Sexual maturity, 5, 6
Snakes, 58
Sodium lactate, 48, 69
'Soft-shell syndrome', 44-47
Soft-shell tortoise, see *M. tornieri*
Steroids, anabolic, 69

147

Worms, see nematodes

X-rays, 64, 66
Xerobates agassizi, 49, 82–85
– and epidemics, 121
– taxonomy, 82

– in captivity, 83
Xerobates berlandieri, 82–85

Yoghurt, live, 57
Yolk, chelonian egg, 14
Yolk-sac, and hatchlings, 28